ANCIENT INDIA

ANCIENT INDIA

AS DESCRIBED BY

MEGASTHENES AND ARRIAN;

BEING

A translation of the Fragments of the Indika of Megasthenes Collected by Dr. Schwanbeck, and of the first Part of the Indika of arrian,

by

J. W. McCRINDLE, M.A.

GYAN

Published by

GYAN

Gyan Publishing House
5, Ansari Road
Daryaganj, New Delhi-110002
Phone: 011-47034999, 9811692060
E-mail: books@gyanbooks.com

Distribution Network
gyanbooks.com
India, USA, Canada, UK, Australia, France

ISBN : 978-81-212-9949-7 (HB)
First Published, 1877

2nd Impression 2021

Printed at: Gyan Press, Delhi.

Ancient India
Author: J. W. McCrindle

ANCIENT INDIA

AS DESCRIBED BY

MEGASTHENÊS AND ARRIAN;

BEING

A TRANSLATION OF THE FRAGMENTS OF THE INDIKA OF MEGASTHENÊS COLLECTED BY DR. SCHWANBECK, AND OF THE FIRST PART OF THE INDIKA OF ARRIAN,

BY

J. W. McCRINDLE, M.A.,

PRINCIPAL OF THE GOVERNMENT COLLEGE, PATNA.
MEMBER OF THE GENERAL COUNCIL OF THE UNIVERSITY OF EDINBURGH,
FELLOW OF THE UNIVERSITY OF CALCUTTA.

WITH INTRODUCTION, NOTES, AND MAP OF ANCIENT INDIA.

Reprinted (with additions) from the "Indian Antiquary," 1876-77.

Calcutta:
THACKER, SPINK & Co.

Bombay:
THACKER & Co.

London:
TRÜBNER & Co.

1877.

PREFACE.

THE account of India written by Megasthenês from his personal knowledge of the country is justly held to be almost invaluable for the light which it throws upon the obscurity of early Indian history. Though, unfortunately, not extant in its original form, it has nevertheless been partially preserved by means of epitomes and quotations to be found scattered up and down the writings of various ancient authors, both Greek and Roman. Dr. Schwanbeck, of Bonn, rendered historical literature a good service by collecting and arranging in their proper order these detached fragments. The work thus reconstructed, and entitled *Megasthenis Indica,* has now been before the world for upwards of thirty years. It has not, however, so far as I know, been as yet translated, at least into our language, and hence it is but little known beyond the circles of the learned. The translation now offered, which goes forth from the very birthplace of the original work, will therefore for the first time place it within the reach of the general public.

A translation of the first part of the *Indika* of Arrian has been subjoined, both because it gives in a connected form a general description of India, and because that description was based chiefly on the work of Megasthenês.

The notes, which turn for the most part on points of history, geography, archæology, and the identification of Greek proper names with their Sanskrit originals, sum up the views of the best and most recent authorities who have written on these subjects. This feature of the work will, I hope, recommend it to the attention of native scholars who may be pursuing, or at least be interested in, inquiries which relate to the history and antiquities of their own country.

In the spelling of classical proper names I have followed throughout the system of Grote, except only in translating from Latin, when the common orthography has been employed.

In conclusion, I may inform my readers that I undertook the present work intending to follow it up with others of a similar kind, until the entire series of classical works relating to India should be translated into the language of its rulers. In furtherance of this design a translation of the short treatise called *The Circumnavigation of the Erythræan Sea,* which gives an account of the ancient commerce of Egypt, Arabia, and India, is nearly ready for publication, and this will be followed by a translation of the narratives of the Makedonian Invasion of India as given by Arrian and Curtius in their respective Histories of Alexander.

CONTENTS.

THE INDIKA OF ARRIAN.

TRANSLATION

OF THE

FRAGMENTS OF THE INDIKA OF MEGASTHENÊS.

COLLECTED BY

DR. E. A. SCHWANBECK : Bonn, 1846.

THE FRAGMENTS OF THE INDIKA OF MEGASTHENÊS.

INTRODUCTION.

The ancient Greeks, till even a comparatively late period in their history, possessed little, if any, real knowledge of India. It is indeed scarcely so much as mentioned by name in their greatest poets, whether epic, lyric, or dramatic. They must, however, have known of its existence as early as the heroic times, for we find from Homer that they used even then articles of Indian merchandize, which went among them by names of Indian origin, such as *kassiteros*, tin, and *elephas*, ivory.* But their conception of it, as we gather from the same source, was vague in the extreme. They imagined it to be an Eastern Ethiopia which stretched away to the uttermost verge of the world, and which, like the Ethiopia of the West, was inhabited by a race of men whose visages were scorched black by the

---

* *Kassiteros* represents the Sanskṛit *kastîra*, 'tin,' a metal found in abundance in the islands, on the coast of India; and *elephas* is undoubtedly connected with *ibha*, the Sanskṛit name for the domestic elephant—its initial syllable being perhaps the Arabic article.

fierce rays of the sun.† Much lies in a name, and the error made by the Greeks in thus calling India E t h i o p i a led them into the further error of considering as pertinent to both these countries narrations, whether of fact or fiction, which concerned but one of them exclusively. This explains why we find in Greek literature mention of peculiar or fabulous races, both of men and other animals, which existed apparently in duplicate, being represented sometimes as located in India, and sometimes in Ethiopia or the countries thereto adjacent.‡ We can hardly wonder, when we consider the distant and sequestered situation of India, that the first conceptions which the Greeks had of it should have been of this nebulous character, but it seems some-

---

† See Homer, *Od.* I. 23-24, where we read

Αἰθίοπες, τοὶ διχθὰ δεδαίαται, ἔσχατοι ἀνδρῶν,
Οἱ μὲν δυσομένου Ὑπερίονος οἱ δ' ἀνιόντος.

(The Ethiopians, who are divided into two, and live at the world's end—one part of them towards the setting sun, the other towards the rising.) Herodotos in several passages mentions the Eastern Ethiopians, but distinguishes them from the Indians (see particularly bk. vii. 70). Ktêsias, however, who wrote somewhat later than Herodotos, frequently calls the Indians by the name of Ethiopians, and the final discrimination between the two races was not made till the Makedonian invasion gave the Western world more correct views of India. Alexander himself, as we learn from Strabo, on first reaching the Indus mistook it for the Nile.

‡ Instances in point are the Skiapodes, Kynamolgoi, Pygmaiôi, Psylloi, Himantopodes, Sternophthalmoi, Makrobioi, and the Makrokephaloi, the Martikhora, and the Krokotta.

what remarkable that they should have learned hardly anything of importance regarding it from the expeditions which were successively undertaken against it by the Egyptians under Sesostris, the Assyrians under Semiramis, and the Persians first under Kyros and afterwards under Dareios the son of Hystaspês.§ Perhaps, as Dr. Robertson has observed, they disdained, through pride of their own superior enlightenment, to pay attention to the transactions of people whom they considered as barbarians, especially in countries far remote from their own. But, in whatever way the fact may be accounted for, India continued to be to the Greeks little better than a land of mystery and fable till the times of the Persian wars, when for the first time they became distinctly aware of its existence. The first historian who speaks clearly of it is Hekataios of Miletos (B.C. 549-486),||

§ Herodotos mentions that Dareios, before invading India, sent Skylax the Karyandian on a voyage of discovery down the Indus, and that Skylax accordingly, setting out from Kaspatyras and the Paktyikan district, reached the mouth of that river, whence he sailed through the Indian Ocean to the Red Sea, performing the whole voyage in thirty months. A little work still extant, which briefly describes certain countries in Europe, Asia, and Africa, bears the name of this Skylax, but from internal evidence it has been inferred that it could not have been written before the reign of Philip of Makedonia, the father of Alexander the Great.

|| The following names pertaining to India occur in Hekataios:—the *Indus*; the *Opiai, a race on the banks of the Indus*; the *Kalatiai, an Indian race*; *Kaspapyros, a Gandaric city*; *Argantê, a city of India*; the *Skiapodes*, and probably the *Pygmies*.

and fuller accounts are preserved in Herodotos¶ and in the remains of Ktêsias, who, having lived for some years in Persia as private physician to king Artaxerxes Mnêmôn, collected materials during his stay for a treatise on India, the first work on the subject written in the Greek language.* His descriptions were, unfortunately, vitiated by a large intermixture of fable, and it was left to the followers of Alexander to give to the Western world for the first time fairly accurate accounts of the country and its inhabitants. The great conqueror, it is well known, carried scientific men with him to chronicle his achievements, and describe the countries to which he might carry his arms, and some of his officers were also men of literary culture, who could wield the pen as well as

---

¶ Herodotos mentions the *river* (Indus), the *Paktyikan district*, the *Gandarioi*, the *Kalantiai* or *Kalatiai*, and the *Padaioi*. Both Hekataios and Herodotos agree in stating that there were sandy deserts in India.

* "The few particulars appropriate to India, and consistent with truth, obtained by Ctêsias, are almost confined to something resembling a description of the cochineal plant, the fly, and the beautiful tint obtained from it, with a genuine picture of the monkey and the parrot; the two animals he had doubtless seen in Persia, and flowered cottons emblazoned with the glowing colours of the modern chintz were probably as much coveted by the fair Persians in the harams of Susa and Ecbatana as they still are by the ladies of our own country; . . . . but we are not bound to admit his fable of the Martichora, his pygmies, his men with the heads of dogs, and feet reversed, his griffins, and his four-footed birds as big as wolves."—*Vincent*.

the sword. Hence the expedition produced quite a crop of narratives and memoirs relating to India, such as those of Baeto, Diognetos, Nearchos, Onesikritos, Aristobulos, Kallisthenês, and others. These works are all lost, but their substance is to be found condensed in Strabo, Pliny, and Arrian. Subsequent to these writers were some others, who made considerable additions to the stock of information regarding India, among whom may be mentioned Dêimachos, who resided for a long time in Palibothra, whither he was sent on an embassy by Seleukos to Allitrochadês, the successor of Sandrakottos; Patroklês, the admiral of Seleukos, who is called by Strabo the least mendacious of all writers concerning India; Timosthenês, admiral of the fleet of Ptolemaios Philadelphos; and Megasthenês, who being sent by Seleukos Nikator on an embassy to Sandrakottos (Chandragupta),† the king of the Prasii, whose capital was Palibothra (Pâṭaliputra, now Pâṭnâ), wrote a work on India of such ackuowledged worth that it formed the principal source whence succeeding writers drew their accounts of the country. This work, which appears

---

† The discovery that the Sandrokottos of the Greeks was identical with the Chandragupta who figures in the Sanskṛit annals and the Sanskṛit drama was one of great moment, as it was the means of connecting Greek with Sanskṛit literature, and of thereby supplying for the first time a date to early Indian history, which had not a single chronological landmark of its own. Diodôros distorts the name into Xandrames, and this again is distorted by Curtius into Agrammes.

to have been entitled τὰ Ἰνδικά, no longer exists, but it has been so often abridged and quoted by the ancient writers that we have a fair knowledge of its contents and their order of arrangement. Dr. Schwanbeck, with great industry and learning, has collected all the fragments that have been anywhere preserved, and has prefixed to the collection a Latin Introduction, wherein, after showing what knowledge the Greeks had acquired of India before Megasthenês, he enters into an examination of those passages in ancient works from which we derive all the little we know of Megasthenês and his Indian mission. He then reviews his work on India, giving a summary of its contents, and, having estimated its value and authority, concludes with a notice of those authors who wrote on India after his time.‡ I have translated in the latter part of the sequel a few instructive passages from this Introduction, one particularly which successfully vindicates Megasthenês from the charge of mendacity so frequently preferred against him. Meanwhile the following extracts, translated from C. Müller's Preface to his edition of the *Indika*, will place before the reader all the information that can be gleaned regarding Megasthenês and his embassy from a careful scrutiny and comparison of all the ancient texts which relate thereto.

Justinus (XV. 4) says of Seleukos Nikator,

‡ He enumerates Eratosthenês, Hipparchos, Polemo, Mnaseos, Apollodôros, Agatharchidês, Alexander Polyhistor, Strabo, Marînos of Tyre, and Ptolemy among the Greeks, and P. Terentius Varro of Atax, M. Vipsanius Agrippa, Pomponius Mela, Seneca, Pliny, and Solinus among the Romans.

'He *carried on many wars in the East after the division* of the Makedonian kingdom between himself and the other successors of Alexander, first seizing Babylonia, and then reducing Baktrianê, his power being increased by the first success. Thereafter he passed into India, which had, since Alexander's death, killed its governors, thinking thereby to shake off from its neck the yoke of slavery. Sandrokottos had made it free: but when victory was gained he changed the name of freedom to that of bondage, for he himself oppressed with servitude the very people which he had rescued from foreign dominion . . . Sandrokottos, having thus gained the crown, held India at the time when Seleukos was laying the foundations of his future greatness. Seleukos came to an agreement with him, and, after settling affairs in the East, engaged in the war against Antigonos (302 B.C.).'

"Besides Justinus, Appianus (*Syr.* c. 55) makes mention of the war which Seleukos had with Sandrokottos or Chandragupta king of the Prasii, or, as they are called in the Indian language, Prâchyas*:—'He (Seleu-

* The adjective πραξιακός in Ælianus *On the Nature of Animals*, xvii. 39 (Megasthen. Fragm. 13. *init.*) bears a very close resemblance to the Indian word Prâchyas (that is 'dwellers in the East'). The substantive would be Πράξιοι, and Schwanbeck (*Megasthenis Indica*, p. 82) thinks that this reading should probably be restored in Stephanus of Byzantium, where the MSS. exhibit Πράσιοι, a form intermediate between Πράξιλος and Πρᾶς. But they are called Πράσιοι by Strabo, Arrianus, and Plinius; Πραίσιοι in Plutarch (*Alex.* chap. 62), and frequently in Ælianus; Πραΰσιοι by Nicolaüs of Damascus, and in the *Florilegium* of Stobæus, 37, 38; Βρείσιοι and Βραίσιοι are the

kos) crossed the Indus and waged war on Sandrokottos, king of the Indians who dwelt about it, until he made friends and entered into relations of marriage with him.' So also Strabo (xv. p. 724) :—' Seleukos Nikator gave to Sandrokottos' (*sc.* a large part of Arianê). Conf. p. 689 :—' The Indians afterwards held a large part of Arianê, (which they had received from the Makedonians), 'entering into marriage relations with him, and receiving in return five hundred elephants' (of which Sandrakottos had nine thousand—Plinius, vi. 22-5); and Plutarch, *Alex.* 62 :—'For not long after, A n d r o k o t t o s, being king, presented Seleukos with five hundred elephants, and with six hundred thousand men attacked and subdued all India.' Phylarchos (Fragm. 28) in Athenæus, p. 18 D., refers to some other wonderful enough presents as being sent to Seleukos by Sandrokottos.

" D i o d o r u s (lib. xx.), in setting forth the affairs of Seleukos, has not said a single word about the Indian war. But it would be strange that that expedition should be mentioned so incidentally by other historians, if it were true, as many recent writers have contended, that Seleukos in this war reached the middle of India as far as the G a n g e s and the town P a l i m b o t h r a,—nay, even advanced as far as the mouths of the Ganges, and therefore left Alexander far behind him. This baseless theory has been well refuted by Lassen (*De Pentap. Ind.* 61), by A. G. Schlegel (*Berliner Calender,*

MS. readings in Diodorus, xvii. 93; P h a r r a s i i in Curtius, IX. ii. 3; P r æ s i d æ in Justinus, XII. viii. 9. See note on Fragm. 13.

1829, p. 31 ; yet see Benfey, *Ersch. u. Grüber. Encycl. v. Indien*, p. 67), and quite recently by Schwanbeck, in a work of great learning and value entitled *Megasthenis Indica* (Bonn, 1846). In the first place, Schwanbeck (p. 13) mentions the passage of Justinus (I. ii. 10) where it is said that no one had entered India but Semiramis and Alexander ; whence it would appear that the expedition of Seleukos was considered so insignificant by Trogus as not even to be on a par with the Indian war of Alexander.† Then he says that Arrianus, if he had known of that remote expedition of Seleukos, would doubtless have spoken differently in his *Indika* (c. 5. 4), where he says that Megasthenês did not travel over much of India, 'but yet more than those who invaded it along with Alexander the son of Philip.' Now in this passage the author could have compared Megasthenês much more suitably and easily with Seleukos.‡ I pass over other proofs of less moment, nor

† Moreover, Schwanbeck calls attention (p. 14) to the words of Appianus (i. 1), where when he says, somewhat inaccurately, that Sandrakottos was king of the Indians around the Indus (τῶν περὶ τὸν Ἰνδὸν Ἰνδῶν) he seems to mean that the war was carried on on the boundaries of India. But this is of no importance, for Appianus has τῶν περὶ αὐτὸν Ἰνδῶν, '*of the Indians around it*,' as Schwanbeck himself has written it (p. 13).

‡ The following passage of the Indian comedy *Mudrârâkshasa* seems to favour the Indian expedition :—" Meanwhile Kusumapura (*i.e.* Pâṭaliputrâ, Palimbothra) the city of Chandragupta and the king of the mountain regions, was invested on every side by the Kirâtas, Yavanas, Kambojas, Persians, Baktrians, and the rest." But "that drama" (Schwanbeck, p. 18), "to follow the authority of Wilson, was written in the tenth century after Christ,—certainly ten centuries after Seleukos. When even the Indian historians have no authority in history, what proof can dramas give written

indeed is it expedient to set forth in detail here all the reasons from which it is improbable of itself that the arms of Seleukos ever reached the region of the Ganges. Let us now examine the passage in Plinius which causes many to adopt contrary opinions. Plinius (*Hist. Nat.* vi. 21), after finding from Diognetos and Baeto the distances of the places from Portæ Caspiæ to the Huphasis, the end of Alexander's march, thus proceeds :—'The other journeys made for Seleukos Nikator are as follows :—One hundred and sixty-eight miles to the Hesidrus, and to the river Jomanes as many (some copies add five miles); from thence to the Ganges one hundred and twelve miles. One hundred and nineteen miles to the Rhodophas (others give three hundred and twenty-five miles for this distance). To the town Kalinipaxa one hundred and sixty-seven. Five hundred (others give two hundred and sixty-five miles), and from thence to the confluence of the Jomanes and Ganges six hundred and twenty-five miles (several add thirteen miles), and to the town Palimbothra four hundred and twenty-five. To the mouth of the Ganges six hundred and thirty-eight' (or seven hundred and thirty-eight, to

---

after many centuries? Yavanas, which was also in later times the Indian name for the Greeks, was very anciently the name given to a certain nation which the Indians say dwelt on the north-western boundaries of India; and the same nation (Manu, x. 44) is also numbered with the Kambojas, the Śakas, the Paradas, the Pallavas, and the Kirâtas as being corrupted among the Kshatriyas. (Conf. Lassen, *Zeitschrift für d. Kunde des Morgenlandes*, III. p. 245.) These Yavanas are to be understood in this passage also, where they are mentioned along with those tribes with which they are usually classed.

follow Schwanbeck's correction),—that is, six thousand stadia, as Megasthenês puts it.

"The ambiguous expression *reliqua Seleuco Nicatori peragrata sunt*, translated above as '*the other journeys made for Seleukos Nikator*,' according to Schwanbeck's opinion, contain a dative 'of advantage,' and therefore can bear no other meaning. The reference is to the journeys of Megasthenês, Dêimachos, and Patroklês, whom Seleukos had sent to explore the more remote regions of Asia. Nor is the statement of Plinius in a passage before this more distinct. ('*India*,') *he says*, '*was thrown open not only by the arms of Alexander the Great, and the kings who were his successors, of whom Seleucus and Antiochus even travelled to the Hyrcanian and Caspian seas, Patrocles being commander of their fleet, but all the Greek writers who stayed behind with the Indian kings (for instance, Megasthenes and Dionysius, sent by Philadelphus for that purpose) have given accounts of the military force of each nation.*' Schwanbeck thinks that the words *circumvectis etiam. . . . . . Seleuco et Antiocho et Patrocle* are properly meant to convey nothing but additional confirmation, and also an explanation how *India was opened up by the arms* of the kings who succeeded Alexander."

"The following statements," continues Müller, "contain all that is related about Megasthenês:—

"'Megasthenês the historian, who lived with Seleukos Nikator',—Clem. Alex. p. 132 *Sylb.* (Fragm. 42); 'Megasthenês, who lived with Sibyrtios § the satrap

§ Sibyrtios, according to Diodorus (XVIII. iii. 3), had gained the satrapy of Arachosia in the third year of the

of Arachosia, and who says that he often visited Sandrakottos, king of the Indians, '—Arrian, *Exp. Alex.* V. vi. 2 (Fragm. 2) ;—'To Sandrokottos, to whom Megasthenês came on an embassy,'—Strabo, xv. p. 702 (Fragm. 25) ;—' Megasthenês and Dêimachos were sent on an embassy, the former to Sandrokottos at Palimbothra, the other to A l l i t r o c h a d ê s his son ; and they left accounts of their sojourn in the country,'—Strabo, ii. p. 70' (Fragm. 29 *note*) ; Megasthenês says that he often visited Sandrokottos, the greatest king (*mahâraja :* v. Bohlen, *Alte Indien,* I. p. 19) of the Indians, and Pôros, still greater than he :'—Arrian, *Ind.* c. 5 (Fragm. 24). Add the passage of Plinius, which Solinus (*Polyhistor.* c. 60) thus renders :—' *Megasthenes remained for some time with the Indian kings, and wrote a history of Indian affairs, that he might hand down to posterity a faithful account of all that he had witnessed. Dionysius, who was sent by Philadelphus to put the truth to the test by personal inspection, wrote also as much.*'

" From these sources, then, we gather that Megasthenês|| was the representative of Seleukos

---

114th Olympiad (B.C. 323), and was firmly established in his satrapy by Antipater (Arrianus, *De Success. Alex.* § 86, ed. Didot). He joined Eumenês in 316 (Diod. xix. 14. 6), but being called to account by him he sought safety in flight (*ibid.* XIX. xxiii. 4). After the defeat of Eumenês, Antigonos delivered to him the most troublesome of the Argyraspides (*ibid.* C. xlviii. 3). He must have afterwards joined Seleukos.

|| Bohlen (*Alte Indien,* I. p. 68) says that Megasthenês was a Persian. No one gives this account of him but Annius Viterbiensis, that forger, whom Bohlen appears to have followed. But it is evidently a Greek name. Strabo (v. p. 243 ; comp. Velleius Paterculus, i. 4) mentions a Megasthenês of Chalkis, who is said to have founded Cumæ in Italy along with Hippoklês of Kumê.

at the court of Sibyrtios, satrap of Arachosia, and that he was sent from thence as the king's ambassador to S a n d r o k o t t o s at Palimbothra, and that not once, but frequently—whether to convey to him the presents of Seleukos, or for some other cause. According to the statement of Arrianus, Megasthenês also visited king Pôros, who was (Diod. xix. 14) already dead in 317 B.C. (Olymp. CXV. 4.) These events should not be referred to the period of Seleukos, but they may very easily be placed in the reign of Alexander, as Bohlen (*Alte Indien*, vol. I. p. 68) appears to have believed they should, when he says Megasthenês was one of the companions of Alexander. But the structure of the sentences does not admit of this conclusion. For Arrianus says, 'It appears to me that Megasthenês did not see much of India, but yet more than the companions of Alexander, for he says that he visited Sandrokottos, the greatest king of the Indians, and Pôros, even greater than he (καὶ Πώρῳ ἔτι τούτου μέζονι).' We should be disposed to say, then, that he made a journey on some occasion or other to Pôros, if the obscurity of the language did not lead us to suspect it a corrupt reading. Lassen (*De Pentap*. p. 44) thinks the mention of Pôros a careless addition of a chance transcriber, but I prefer Schwanbeck's opinion, who thinks it should be written καὶ Πώρου ἔτι τούτῳ μέζονι, '*and who was even greater than Pôros*.' If this correction is admitted, everything fits well.

"The time when he discharged his embassy or embassies, and how long he stayed in India, cannot be determined, but he was probably sent after the treaty had been struck and friendship had sprung up between the two kings. If, therefore, we make the reign of Sandrokottos extend to the year 288, Megasthenês would have set out for Palimbothra between 302 and 288. Clinton (*F. H.* vol. III. p. 482) thinks he came to the Indian king a little before B.C. 302."

While the date of the visit of Megasthenês to India is thus uncertain, there is less doubt as to what were the parts of the country which he saw; and on this point Schwanbeck thus writes (p. 21):—

"Both from what he himself says, and because he has enumerated more accurately than any of the companions of Alexander, or any other Greek, the rivers of Kâbul and the Panjâb, it is clear that he had passed through these countries. Then, again, we know that he reached Pâṭaliputra by travelling along the royal road. But he does not appear to have seen more of India than those parts of it, and he acknowledges himself that he knew the lower part of the country traversed by the Ganges only by hearsay and report. It is commonly supposed that he also spent some time in the Indian camp, and therefore in some part of the country, but where cannot now be known. This opinion, however, is based on a corrupt reading which the editions of Strabo exhibit. For in all the MSS. of Strabo (p. 709) is found this reading:—*Γενομένους δ'οὖν 'εν τῷ Σανδροκόττου στρατοπέδῳ φησὶν ὁ Μεγασθένης, τετταράκοντα μυριάδων πλήθους ἱδρυμένου, μηδεμίαν ἡμέραν ἰδεῖν ἀνηνεγμένα κλέμματα πλειόνων ἢ διακοσίων δραχμῶν ἄξια.* 'Megasthenês says that those who were in the camp of Sandrokottos saw,' &c. From this translation that given by Guarini and Gregorio alone is different. They render thus :—'Megasthenes refert, quum in Sandrocotti castra venisset . . . vidisse,' 'Megasthenês relates that when he had come into the camp of Sandrokottos, he saw,' &c. From this it appears that the translator had found written γενόμενος. But since that translation is hardly equal in authority even to a single MS., and since the word γενομένους can be changed more readily into the word γενόμενος than γενόμενος into γενομένους, there is no reason at all why we should depart from the reading of all the MSS., which Casaubon disturbed by a baseless conjecture, contending that γενόμενος should be substituted,—inasmuch as it is evident from Strabo and Arrianus (V. vi. 2) that Megasthenês had been sent to Sandrokottos,—which is an argument utterly futile. Nevertheless from the time of Casaubon the wrong reading γενόμενος which he promulgated has held its ground."

That Megasthenês paid more than one visit to India Schwanbeck is not at all inclined to believe. On this point he says (p. 23)—

"That Megasthenês frequently visited India recent writers, all with one consent, following Robertson, are wont to maintain ; nevertheless this opinion is far from being certain. For what Arrianus has said in his *Exped. Alex.* V. vi. 2,—Πολλάκις δὲ λέγει (Μεγασθένης) ἀφικέσθαι παρὰ Σανδράκοττον τὸν Ἰνδῶν βασιλέα, does not solve the question, for he might have meant by the words that Megasthenês during his embassy had frequent interviews with Chandragupta. Nor, if we look to the context, does any other explanation seem admissible; and in fact no other writer besides has mentioned his making frequent visits, although occasion for making such mention was by no means wanting, and in the *Indika* itself of Megasthenês not the slightest indication of his having made numerous visits is to be found. But perhaps some may say that to this view is opposed the accurate knowledge which he possessed on all Indian matters; but this may equally well be accounted for by believing that he made a protracted stay at Pâṭaliputra as by supposing that he frequently visited India. Robertson's conjecture appears, therefore, uncertain, not to say hardly credible."

Regarding the veracity of Megasthenês, and his value as a writer, Schwanbeck writes (p. 59) to this effect :—

"The ancient writers, whenever they judge of those who have written on Indian matters, are without doubt wont to reckon Megasthenês among those writers who are given to lying and least worthy of credit, and to rank him almost on a par with Ktêsias. Arrianus alone has judged better of him, and delivers his opinion of him in these words :— 'Regarding the Indians I shall set down in a special work all that is most credible for narration in the accounts penned by those who accompanied Alexander on his expedition, and by Nearchus, who navigated the great sea which washes the shores of India, and also by Megasthenês and Eratosthenês, who are both approved men (δοκίμω ἄνδρε) :' Arr. *Exped. Alex.* V. v.

"The foremost amongst those who disparage him is Eratosthenês, and in open agreement with him are Strabo and Pliny. Others, among whom is Diodorus, by omitting certain particulars related by Megasthenês, sufficiently show that they discredit that part of his narrative.¶

¶ Regarding the manner in which Strabo, Arrianus, Diodorus, and Plinius used the *Indika* of Megasthenês, Schwanbeck remarks:—" Strabo, and—not unlike to Strabo—Arrianus, who, however, gave a much less carefully considered account of India, abridged the descriptions of Megasthenês, yet in such a way that they wrote at once in an agreeable style and with strict regard to accuracy. But when Strabo designed not merely to instruct but also to delight his readers, he omitted whatever would be out of place in an entertaining narrative or picturesque description, and avoided above all things aught that would look like a dry list of names. Now though this may not be a fault, still it is not to be denied that those particulars which he has omitted would have very greatly helped our knowledge of Ancient India. Nay, Strabo, in his eagerness to be interesting, has gone so far that the topography of India is almost entirely a blank in his pages.

" Diodorus, however, in applying this principle of composition has exceeded all bounds. For as he did not aim at writing learnedly for the instruction of others, but in a light, amusing style, so as to be read with delight by the multitude, he selected for extract such parts as best suited this purpose. He has therefore omitted not only the most accurate narrations of fact, but also the fables which his readers might consider as incredible, and has been best pleased to describe instead that part of Indian life which to the Greeks would appear singular and diverting. . . . Nevertheless his epitome is not without its value; for although we do not learn much that is new from its contents, still it has the advantage over all the others of being the most coherent, while at the same time it enables us to attribute with certainty an occasional passage to Megasthenês, which without its help we could but conjecture proceeded from his pen.

"Since Strabo, Arrianus, and Diodorus have directed their attention to relate nearly the same things, it has resulted that the greatest part of the *Indika* has been completely lost, and that of many passages, singularly enough, three epitomes are extant, to which occasionally a fourth is added by Plinius.

"At a great distance from these writers, and especially from Diodorus, stands Plinius: whence it happens that he both differs most from that writer, and also best supplements his epitome. Where the narrative of Strabo and Arrianus is at once pleasing and instructive, and Diodorus charms us with a lively sketch, Pliny gives instead, in the baldest lan-

"Strabo (p. 70) says, 'Generally speaking, the men who have hitherto written on the affairs of India were a set of liars,—Dêimachos holds the first place in the list, Megasthenês comes next; while Onesikritos and Nearchos, with others of the same class, manage to stammer out a few words (of truth). Of this we became the more convinced whilst writing the history of Alexander. No faith whatever can be placed in Dêimachos and Megasthenês. They coined the fables concerning men with ears large enough to sleep in, men without any mouths, without noses, with only one eye, with spider legs, and with fingers bent backward. They renewed Homer's fables concerning the battles of the cranes and pygmies, and asserted the latter to be three spans high. They told of ants digging for gold, and Pans with wedge-shaped heads, of serpents swallowing down oxen and stags, horns and all,—meantime, as Eratosthenês has observed, accusing each other of falsehood. Both of these men were sent as ambassadors to Palimbothra,—Megasthenês to Sandrokottos, Dêimachos to Amitrochadês his son,—and such are the notes of their residence abroad, which, I know not why, they thought fit to leave.

"When he adds, 'Patroklês certainly does not resemble them, nor do any other of the authorities

---

guage, an ill-digested enumeration of names. With his usual wonderful diligence he has written this part, but more frequently still he writes with too little care and judgment,—a fact of which we have already seen numerous instances. In a careless way, as is usual, he commends authors, so that if you compared his accounts of Taprobane and the kingdom of the Prasii you would think that he had lived at different periods. He frequently commends Megasthenês, but more frequently seems to transcribe him without acknowledgment."—pp. 56-58.

consulted by Eratosthenês contain such absurdities,* we may well wonder, seeing that, of all the writers on India, Eratosthenês has chiefly followed Megasthenês. Plinius (*Hist. Nat.* VI. xxi. 3) says: 'India was opened up to our knowledge . . . even by other Greek writers, who, having resided with Indian kings,—as for instance Megasthenês and Dionysius,—made known the strength of the races which peopled the country. It is not, however, worth while to study their accounts with care, so conflicting are they, and incredible.'

"These same writers, however, seeing they have copied into their own pages a great part of his *Indika*, cannot by any means have so entirely distrusted his veracity as one might easily infer they did from these judgments. And what of this, that Eratosthenês himself, who did not quote him sparingly, says in Strabo (p. 689) that "he sets down the breadth of India from the register of the Stathmi, which were received as authentic,'—a passage which can have reference to Megasthenês alone. The fact is they find fault with only two parts of the narrative of Megasthenês,—the one in which he writes of the fabulous races of India, and the other where he gives an account of Heraklês and the Indian Dionysus; although it so happens that on other matters also they regarded the account given by others as true, rather than that of Megasthenês.

"The Âryan Indians were from the remotest period surrounded on all sides by indigenous tribes in a state of barbarism, from whom they differed both in mind and disposition. They were most acutely sensible of this difference, and gave it a very pointed expression. For as barbarians, even by the sanction of the gods themselves, are excluded from the Indian commonwealth, so they seem to have been currently regarded by the Indians as of a nature and disposition lower than their own, and bestial rather than human. A difference existing between minds is not easily perceived, but the Indians were quick to discern how unlike the barbarous tribes were to themselves in bodily figure; and the divergence they exaggerated, making bad worse, and so framed to themselves a mental picture of these tribes beyond measure hideous. When reports in circulation regarding them had given fixity to this conception, the poets seized on it as a basis for further exaggeration, and embellished it with fables. Other races, and these even Indian, since they had originated in an intermixture of tribes, or since they did not sufficiently follow Indian manners, and especially the system of caste, so roused the common hatred of the Indians that they were reckoned in the same category with the barbarians, and represented as equally hideous of aspect. Accordingly in the epic poems we see all Brahmanical India surrounded by races not at all real, but so imaginary that sometimes it cannot be discovered how the fable originated.

"Forms still more wonderful you will find by bestowing a look at the gods of the Indians and their retinue, among whom particularly the attendants of Kuvêra and Kârtikêya are described in such a manner (conf. *Mahábh.* ix. 2558 *et seq*). that hardly anything which it is possible for the human imagination to invent seems omitted. These, however, the Indians now sufficiently distinguish from the fabulous races, since they neither believe that they live within the borders of India, nor have any intercourse with the human race. These, therefore, the Greeks could not confound with the races of India.

"These races, however, might be more readily confounded with other creatures of the Indian imagination, who held a sort of intermediate place between demons and men, and whose number was legion. For the Râkshasas and other Piśâchas are said to have the same characteristics as the fabulous races, and the only difference between them is that, while a single (evil) attribute only is ascribed to each race, many or all of these are assigned to the Râkshasas and the Piśâchas. Altogether so slight is the distinction between the two that any strict lines of demarcation can hardly be drawn between them. For the Râkshasas, though described as very terrible beings, are nevertheless believed to be human, and both to live on the earth and take part in Indian battles, so that an ordinary Indian could hardly define how the nature of a Râkshasa differs from that of a man. There is scarcely any one thing found to characterize the Râkshasas which is not attributed to some race or other. Therefore, although the Greeks might have heard of these by report,—which cannot be proved for certain,—they could scarcely, by reason of that, have erred in describing the manners of the races according to the Indian conception.

"That reports about these tribes should have reached Greece is not to be wondered at. For fables invented with some glow of poetic fervour have a remarkable facility in gaining a wide currency, which is all the greater in proportion to the boldness displayed in their invention. Those fables also in which the Indians have represented the lower animals as talking to each other have been diffused through almost every country in the world, in a way we cannot understand. Other fables found their way to the Greeks before even the name of India was known to them. In this class some fables even in Homer must be reckoned,—a matter which, before the Vedas were better known, admitted only of probable conjecture, but could not be established by unquestionable proofs. We perceive, moreover, that the further the epic poems of the Greeks depart from their original simplicity the more, for that very reason, do those fables creep into them; while a very liberal use of them is made by the poets of a later age. It would be a great mistake to suppose that those fables only in which India is mentioned proceeded from India; for a fable in becoming current carries along with it the name of the locality in which the scene of it is laid. An example will make this clear. The Indians supposed that towards the north, beyond the Himâlaya, dwelt the Uttarakuri, a people who enjoyed a long and happy life, to whom disease and care were unknown, and who revelled in every delight in a land all paradise. This fable made its way to the West, carrying with it the name of the locality to which it related, and so it came to pass that from the time of Hesiod the Greeks supposed that towards the north lived the Hyperboreans, whose very name was fashioned after some likeness to the Indian name. The reason why the Indians placed the seat of this happy people towards the north is manifest; but there was not the slightest reason which can be discovered why the Greeks should have done so. Nay, the locality assigned to the Hyperboreans is not only out of harmony, but in direct conflict, with that conception of the world which the Greeks entertained.

"The first knowledge of the mythical geography of the Indians dates from this period, when the Greeks were the unconscious recipients of Indian fables. Fresh knowledge was imparted by S k y- l a x, who first gave a description of India; and all writers from the time of Skylax, with not a single exception, mention those fabulous races, but in such a way that they are wont to speak of them as Æthiopians; by doing which they have incurred obloquy and the suspicion of dishonesty, especially K t ê s i a s. This writer, however, is not at all untruthful when he says, in the conclusion of his *Indika* (33), that 'he omits many of these stories, and others still more marvellous, that he may not appear, to such as have not seen these, to be telling what is incredible;' for he could have described many other fabulous races, as for example men with the heads of tigers (*vyághramuchás*), others with the necks of snakes (*vyalagrívás*), others having horses' heads (*turanga-vadanás, aśvamuchás*), others with feet like dogs (*śvâpadás*), others with four feet (*chatushpadás*), others with three eyes (*trinêtrás*), and others with six hundred.

"Nor were the companions of Alexander able to disregard these fables,—in fact, scarcely any of them doubted their truth. For, generally speaking, they were communicated to them by the Brâhmaṇs, whose learning and wisdom they held in the utmost veneration. Why, then, should we be surprised that Megasthenês also, following examples so high and numerous, should have handled those fables? His account of them is to be found in Strabo 711; Pliny, *Hist. Nat.* vii. 2. 14-22; Solinus 52." (Sch. p. 64.)

Schwanbeck then examines the fables related by Megasthenês, and having shown that they were of Indian origin, thus proceeds (p. 74):—

"The relative veracity of Megasthenês, then, cannot be questioned, for he related truthfully both what he actually saw, and what was told him by others. If we therefore seek to know what reliance is to be placed on any particular narrative, this other point must be considered, how far his informants were worthy of credit. But here no ground for suspicion exists; for on those matters which did not come under his own observation he had his information from those Brâhmaṇs who were the rulers of the state, to whom he again and again appeals as his authorities. Accordingly he was able not only to describe how the kingdom of the Prasii was governed, but also to give an estimate of the power of other nations and the strength of their armies. Hence we cannot wonder that Indian ideas are to be found in the books of Megasthenês mixed up with accounts of what he personally observed and with Greek ideas.

"Therefore to him, as to the companions of Alexander, it cannot be objected that he told too much. That he did not tell too little to give an adequate account of Indian affairs to Greek readers we know. For he has described the country, its soil, climate, animals, and plants, its government and religion, the manners of its people and their arts,—in short, the whole of Indian life from the king to the remotest tribe; and he has scanned every object with a mind sound and unprejudiced, without overlooking even trifling and minute circumstances. If we see any part omitted, a little only said about the religion and gods of the Indians, and nothing at all about their literature, we should reflect that we are not reading his veritable book, but only an epitome and some particular fragments that have survived the wreck of time." (p. 75.)

"Of the slight mistakes into which he fell, some are of that kind into which even the most careful observer may be betrayed, as for instance his incorrectly stating that the Vipâśa pours its waters into the Irâvati. Others had their origin in his misapprehension of the meaning of Indian words; to which head must be referred his assertion that among the Indians laws were not written, but everything decided by memory. Besides he alleges that on those Brâhmaṇs who had thrice erred in making up the calendar silence for the rest of their lives was enjoined as a punishment. This passage, which has not yet been cleared up, I would explain by supposing that he had heard the Indian word *mâunin*, a name which is applied both to a taciturn person and to any ascetic. Finally, some errors had their source in this, that he looked at Indian matters from a Greek's point of view, from which it resulted that he did not correctly enumerate the castes, and gave a mistaken account of the Indian gods and other matters.

"Notwithstanding, the work of Megasthenês—in so far as it is a part of Greek literature and of Greek and Roman learning—is, as it were, the culmination of the knowledge which the ancients ever acquired of India: for although the geographical science of the Greeks attained afterwards a perfect form, nevertheless the knowledge of India derived from the books of Megasthenês has only approached perfect accuracy the more closely those who have written after him on India have followed his *Indika.* And it is not only on account of his own merit that Megasthenês is a writer of great importance, but also on this other ground, that while other writers have borrowed a great part of what they relate from him, he exercised a powerful influence on the whole sphere of Latin and Greek scientific knowledge.

"Besides this authority which the *Indika* of Megasthenês holds in Greek literature, his remains have another value, since they hold not the last place among the sources whence we derive our knowledge of Indian antiquity. For as there now exists a knowledge of our own of ancient India, still on some points he increases the knowledge which we have acquired from other sources, even though his narrative not seldom requires to be supplemented and corrected. Notwithstanding, it must be conceded that the new information we have learned from him is neither extremely great in amount nor weight. What is of greater importance than all that is new in what he has told us, is—that he has recalled a picture of the condition of India at a definite period,—a service of all the greater value, because Indian literature, always self-consistent, is wont to leave us in the greatest doubt if we seek to know what happened at any particular time." (pp. 76, 77.)

It is yet an unsettled question whether the *Indika* was written in the Attic or the Ionic dialect.*

---

* The following authorities are quoted by Schwanbeck (pp. 23, 24) to show that the *Indika* of Megasthenês was divided into four books:—Athen. IV. p. 153—where the 2nd book is mentioned; Clem. Alex. *Strom.* I. p. 132 Sylb., where the 3rd book is mentioned; Joseph. *contra Apion*, I. 20, and *Antiq. Jud.* X. xi. 1, where the 4th book is mentioned—cf. G. Syncell. tom. I. p. 419, Bonn. The assignment of the fragments to their respective books was a matter of some difficulty, as the order of their connection varies in different authors.

FRAGMENT I.,

OR AN EPITOME OF MEGASTHENÊS.

(Diod. II. 35-42.)

(35.) [1]India, which is in shape quadrilateral, has its eastern as well as its western side bounded by the great sea, but on the northern side it is divided by Mount Hemôdos from that part of Skythia which is inhabited by those Skythians who are called the Sakai, while the fourth or western side is bounded by the river called the Indus, which is perhaps the largest of all rivers in the world after the Nile. [2]The extent of the whole country from east to west is said to be 28,000 stadia, and from north to south 32,000. [3]Being thus of such vast extent, it seems well-nigh to embrace the whole of the northern tropic zone of the earth, and in fact at the extreme point of India the gnomon of the sundial may frequently be observed to cast no shadow, while the constellation of the Bear is by night invisible, and in the remotest parts even Arcturus disappears from view. Consistently with this, it is also stated that shadows there fall to the southward.

[4]India has many huge mountains which abound in fruit-trees of every kind, and many vast plains of great fertility—more or less beautiful,

---

[1] With Epit. 1, conf. Fragm. ii., iii. (in *Ind. Ant.* vol. V. p. 86, c. 2).

[1-2] Conf. Fragm. iv. [3] Conf. Fragm. ix.

but all alike intersected by a multitude of rivers. [5] The greater part of the soil, moreover, is under irrigation, and consequently bears two crops in the course of the year. It teems at the same time with animals of all sorts,—beasts of the field and fowls of the air,—of all different degrees of strength and size. [6] It is prolific, besides, in elephants, which are of monstrous bulk, as its soil supplies food in unsparing profusion, making these animals far to exceed in strength those that are bred in Libya. It results also that, since they are caught in great numbers by the Indians and trained for war, they are of great moment in turning the scale of victory.

(36.) [7] The inhabitants, in like manner, having abundant means of subsistence, exceed in consequence the ordinary stature, and are distinguished by their proud bearing. They are also found to be well skilled in the arts, as might be expected of men who inhale a pure air and drink the very finest water. [8] And while the soil bears on its surface all kinds of fruits which are known to cultivation, it has also under ground numerous veins of all sorts of metals, for it contains much gold and silver, and copper and iron in no small quantity, and even tin and other metals, which are employed in making articles of use and ornament, as well as the implements and accoutrements of war.

[9] In addition to cereals, there grows throughout

[5-9] Conf. Fragm. xi.

India much millet, which is kept well watered by the profusion of river-streams, and much pulse of different sorts, and rice also, and what is called *bosporum*, as well as many other plants useful for food, of which most grow spontaneously. [10] The soil yields, moreover, not a few other edible products fit for the subsistence of animals, about which it would be tedious to write. It is accordingly affirmed that famine has never visited India, and that there has never been a general scarcity in the supply of nourishing food. [11] For, since there is a double rainfall in the course of each year,—one in the winter season, when the sowing of wheat takes place as in other countries, and the second at the time of the summer solstice, which is the proper season for sowing rice and *bosporum*, as well as sesamum and millet—the inhabitants of India almost always gather in two harvests annually; and even should one of the sowings prove more or less abortive they are always sure of the other crop. [12] The fruits, moreover, of spontaneous growth, and the esculent roots which grow in marshy places and are of varied sweetness, afford abundant sustenance for man. [13] The fact is, almost all the plains in the country have a moisture which is alike genial, whether it is derived from the rivers, or from the rains of the summer season, which are wont to fall every year at a stated period with surprising regularity; while the great heat which prevails ripens the roots which grow in the marshes, and especially those of the tall reeds.

[14] But, further, there are usages observed by the Indians which contribute to prevent the occurrence of famine among them; for whereas among other nations it is usual, in the contests of war, to ravage the soil, and thus to reduce it to an uncultivated waste, among the Indians, on the contrary, by whom husbandmen are regarded as a class that is sacred and inviolable, the tillers of the soil, even when battle is raging in their neighbourhood, are undisturbed by any sense of danger, for the combatants on either side in waging the conflict make carnage of each other, but allow those engaged in husbandry to remain quite unmolested. Besides, they neither ravage an enemy's land with fire, nor cut down its trees.

(37.) [15] India, again, possesses many rivers both large and navigable, which, having their sources in the mountains which stretch along the northern frontier, traverse the level country, and not a few of these, after uniting with each other, fall into the river called the Ganges. [16] Now this river, which at its source is 30 stadia broad, flows from north to south, and empties its waters into the ocean forming the eastern boundary of the Gangaridai, a nation which possesses a vast force of the largest-sized elephants. [17] Owing to this, their country has never been conquered by any foreign king: for all other nations dread the overwhelming number and strength of these animals. [18] [Thus Alexander the Makedonian, after conquering all Asia, did not make war upon the Gangaridai,† as he did on all others; for when he had arrived with all his troops at the river Ganges, and had subdued all the other Indians, he abandoned as hopeless an invasion of the Gangaridai when he learned that they possessed four thousand elephants well trained and equipped for war.] [19]Another river, about the same size as the Ganges, called the I n d u s, has its sources, like its rival, in the north, and falling into the ocean forms *on its way* the boundary of India; in its passage through the vast stretch of level country it receives not a few tributary streams which are navigable, the most notable of them being the H u p a n i s, the H u d a s p ê s, and the A k e s i n ê s. Besides these rivers there are a great many others of every description, which permeate the country, and supply water for the nurture of garden vegetables and crops of all sorts. [20]Now to account for the rivers being so numerous, and the supply of water so superabundant, the native philosophers and proficients in natural science advance the following reasons:—They

---

† Conf. Lassen, *Pentapot.* 16.

[21] Conf. Fragm. xxi. in *Ind. Ant.* vol. V. p. 88, c. vi. 2-3.

[18-19] Conf. Fragm. xx. in *Ind. Ant.* vol. V. p. 87, c. iv. 2-13.

say that the countries which surround India—those of the Skythians and Baktrians, and also of the Âryans—are more elevated than India, so that their waters, agreeably to natural law, flow down together from all sides to the plains beneath, where they gradually saturate the soil with moisture, and generate a multitude of rivers.

[21] A peculiarity is found to exist in one of the rivers of India,—that called the Sillas, which flows from a fountain bearing the same name. It differs from all other rivers in this respect,—that nothing cast into it will float, but everything, strange to say, sinks down to the bottom.

(38.) [22]It is said that India, being of enormous size when taken as a whole, is peopled by races both numerous and diverse, of which not even one was originally of foreign descent, but all were evidently indigenous; [23]and moreover that India neither received a colony from abroad, nor sent out a colony to any other nation. [24] The legends further inform us that in primitive times the inhabitants subsisted on such fruits as the earth yielded spontaneously, and were clothed with the skins of the beasts found in the country, as was the case with the Greeks; and that, in like manner *as with them*, the arts and other appliances which improve human life were gradually invented, Necessity herself teaching

---

[22] Conf. Fragm. xlvi.

them to an animal at once docile and furnished not only with hands ready to second all his efforts, but also with reason and a keen intelligence.

[38] The men of greatest learning among the Indians tell certain legends, of which it may be proper to give a brief summary.‡ They relate that in the most primitive times, when the people of the country were still living in villages, D i o n u s o s made his appearance coming from the regions lying to the west, and at the head of a considerable army. He over-

‡ FRAGM. I. B. Diod. III. 63.

Concerning Dionusos.

Now some, as I have already said, supposing that there were three individuals of this name, who lived in different ages, assign to each appropriate achievements. They say, then, that the most ancient of them was I n d o s, and that as the country, with its genial temperature, produced spontaneously the vine-tree in great abundance, he was the first who crushed grapes and discovered the use of the properties of wine. In like manner he ascertained what culture was requisite for figs and other fruit trees, and transmitted this knowledge to after-times; and, in a word, it was he who found out how these fruits should be gathered in, whence also he was called L ê n a i o s. This same Dionusos, however, they call also K a t a p ô g ô n, since it is a custom among the Indians to nourish their beards with great care to the very end of

ran the whole of India, as there was no great city capable of resisting his arms. [26] The heat, however, having become excessive, and the soldiers of Dionusos being afflicted with a pestilence, the leader, who was remarkable for his sagacity, carried his troops away from the plains up to the hills. There the army, recruited by the cool breezes and the waters that flowed fresh from the fountains, recovered from sickness. [27] The place among the mountains where Dionusos restored his troops to health was called M ê r o s; from which cir-

---

their life. Dionusos then, at the head of an army, marched to every part of the world, and taught mankind the planting of the vine, and how to crush grapes in the winepress, whence he was called L ê n a i o s. Having in like manner imparted to all a knowledge of his other inventions, he obtained after his departure from among men immortal honour from those who had benefited by his labours. It is further said that the place is pointed out in India even to this day where the god had been, and that cities are called by his name in the vernacular dialects, and that many other important evidences still exist of his having been born in India, about which it would be tedious to write.

---

[26] *et seqq.* Conf. Fragm. lvii.

[26-28] Conf. Fragm. l. in *Ind. Ant.* vol. V. p. 89, c. vii.—"He tells us further," &c. to c. viii.—" on the principle of merit."

cumstance, no doubt, the Greeks have transmitted to posterity the legend concerning the god, that Dionusos was bred in *his father's thigh.*§ [28] Having after this turned his attention to the artificial propagation of useful plants, he communicated the secret to the Indians, and taught them the way to make wine, as well as other arts conducive to human well-being. [29] He was, besides, the founder of large cities, which he formed by removing the villages to convenient sites, while he also showed the people how to worship the deity, and introduced laws and courts of justice. [30] Having thus achieved altogether many great and noble works, he was regarded as a deity and gained immortal honours. It is related also of him that he led about with his army a great host of women, and employed, in marshalling his troops for battle, drums and cymbals, as the trumpet had not in his days been invented; [31] and that after reigning over the whole of India for two and fifty years he died of old age, while his sons, succeeding to the government, transmitted the sceptre in unbroken succession to their posterity. [32] At last, after many generations had come and gone, the sovereignty, it is said, was dissolved, and democratic governments were set up in the cities.

(39.) [33] Such, then, are the traditions regarding Dionusos and his descendants current

---

§ μηρός. [32] Conf. Fragm. li.

among the Indians who inhabit the hill-country. [34] They further assert that H e r a k l ê s|| also was born among them. [34] They assign to him, like the Greeks, the club and the lion's skin. He far surpassed other men in personal strength and prowess, and cleared sea and land of evil beasts. [35] Marrying many wives he begot many sons, but one daughter only. The sons having reached man's estate, he divided all India into equal portions for his children, whom he made kings in different parts of his dominions. He provided similarly for his only daughter, whom he reared up and made a queen. [36] He was the founder, also, of no small number of cities, the most renowned and greatest of which he called P a l i b o t h r a. He built therein many sumptuous palaces, and settled within its walls a numerous population. The city he fortified with trenches of notable dimensions, which were filled with water introduced from the river. [37] Heraklês, accordingly, after his removal from among men, obtained immortal honour; and his descendants, having reigned for many generations and signalized themselves by great achievements, neither made any expedition beyond the confines of India, nor sent out any colony abroad. [38] At

---

[34-35] Conf. Fragm. l. in *Ind. Ant.* vol. V. pp. 89-90, c. viii., from " But that Hercules," &c. to " of his daughter."

|| Apparently Ś i v a is meant, though his *many* wives and sons are unknown to Hindu mythology.—Ed.

[36] Conf. Fragm. xxv.

last, however, after many years had gone, most of the cities adopted the democratic form of government, though some retained the kingly until the invasion of the country by A l e x a n- d e r. [39] Of several remarkable customs existing among the Indians, there is one prescribed by their ancient philosophers which one may regard as truly admirable: for the law ordains that no one among them shall, under any circumstances, be a slave, but that, enjoying freedom, they shall respect the equal right to it which all possess: for those, *they thought*, who have learned neither to domineer over nor to cringe to others will attain the life best adapted for all vicissitudes of lot: for it is but fair and reasonable to institute laws which bind all equally, but allow property to be unevenly distributed.

(40.) The whole population of India is divided into seven castes, of which the *first* is formed by the collective body of the P h i l o s o p h e r s,¶ which in point of number is inferior to the other classes, but in point of dignity preëminent over all. For the philosophers, being exempted from all public duties, are neither the masters nor the servants of others. [41] They are, however, engaged by private persons to offer the sacrifices due in lifetime, and to celebrate the obsequies of

---

¶ Φιλόσοφοι, Strabo, Diod. Σοφισταί, Arr.

[40-53] Conf. Fragm. xxxii. in *Ind. Ant.* vol. V. pp. 91-92, cc. xi. and xii.

the dead: for they are *believed* to be most dear to the gods, and to be the most conversant with matters pertaining to Hades. In requital of such services they receive valuable gifts and privileges. [42] To the people of India at large they also render great benefits, when, gathered together at the beginning of the year, they forewarn the assembled multitudes about droughts and wet weather, and also about propitious winds, and diseases, and other topics capable of profiting the hearers. [43] Thus the people and the sovereign, learning beforehand what is to happen, always make adequate provision against a coming deficiency, and never fail to prepare beforehand what will help in a time of need. The philosopher who errs in his predictions incurs no other penalty than obloquy, and he then observes silence for the rest of his life.

[44] The *second* caste consists of the Husbandmen,* who appear to be far more numerous than the others. Being, moreover, exempted from fighting and other public services, they devote the whole of their time to tillage; nor would an enemy coming upon a husbandman at work on his land do him any harm, for men of this class, being regarded as public benefactors, are protected from all injury. The land, thus remaining unravaged, and producing heavy crops, supplies the inhabitants with all that is

* Γεωργοί, Strab. Arr. Diod.

requisite to make life very enjoyable. [45] The husbandmen themselves, with their wives and children, live in the country, and entirely avoid going into town. [46] They pay a land-tribute to the king, because all India is the property of the crown, and no private person is permitted to own land. Besides the land-tribute, they pay into the royal treasury a fourth part of the produce of the soil.

[47] The *third* caste consists of the Neatherds and Shepherds,† and in general of all herdsmen who neither settle in towns nor in villages, but live in tents. By hunting and trapping they clear the country of noxious birds and wild beasts. As they apply themselves eagerly and assiduously to this pursuit, they free India from the pests with which it abounds,—all sorts of wild beasts, and birds which devour the seeds sown by the husbandmen.‡

(41.) [48] The *fourth* caste consists of the Artizans.§ Of these some are armourers, while others make the implements which husbandmen and others find useful in their different callings. This class is not only exempted from paying

---

† Βουκόλοι καὶ ποιμένες καὶ καθόλου πάντες οἱ νομέες, Diod. Ποιμένες καὶ θηρευταί, Strab. Ποιμένες τε καὶ βουκόλοι, Arr.

‡ Shepherds and hunters were not a caste of Hindûs, but were probably tribes like the Abhirs or Ahîrs, Dhangars, &c.—Ed.

§ Τεχνῖται.

taxes, but even receives maintenance from the royal exchequer.

[49] The *fifth* caste is the Military.|| It is well organized and equipped for war, holds the second place in point of numbers, and gives itself up to idleness and amusement in the times of peace. The entire force—men-at-arms, war-horses, war-elephants, and all—are maintained at the king's expense.

[50] The *sixth* caste consists of the Overseers. It is their province to inquire into and superintend all that goes on in India, and make report to the king,¶ or, where there is not a king, to the magistrates.

[51] The *seventh* caste consists of the Councillors and Assessors,—of those who deliberate on public affairs. It is the smallest class, looking to number, but the most respected, on account of the high character and wisdom of its members; [52] for from their ranks the advisers of the king are taken, and the treasurers of the state, and the arbiters who settle disputes. The generals of the army also, and the chief magistrates, usually belong to this class.

[53] Such, then, are about the parts into which the body politic in India is divided. No one is allowed to marry out of his own caste, or to

---

|| Πολεμισταί, Strab. Arr.

¶ Ἔφοροι, Diod. Strab. Ἐπίσκοποι, Arr. Is this the class of officers referred to as sheriffs—*mahâmatra*—in the Aśoka inscriptions? Conf. *Ind. Ant.* vol. V. pp. 267-8.—Ed.

exercise any calling or art except his own: for instance, a soldier cannot become a husbandman, or an artizan a philosopher.*

(42.) [54] India possesses a vast number of huge elephants, which far surpass *those found elsewhere* both in strength and size. This animal does not cover the female in a peculiar way, as some affirm, but like horses and other quadrupeds. [55] The period of gestation is at shortest sixteen months, and at furthest eighteen.† Like mares, they generally bring forth but one young one at a time, and this the dam suckles for six years. [56] Most elephants live to be as old as an extremely old man, but the most aged live two hundred years.

[57] Among the Indians officers are appointed even for foreigners, whose duty is to see that no foreigner is wronged. Should any of them lose his health, they send physicians to attend him, and take care of him otherwise, and if he dies they bury him, and deliver over such property as he leaves to his relatives. [58] The judges

---

* "It appears strange that Megasthenês should have divided the people of India into seven castes . . . Herodotus, however, had divided the people of Egypt into seven castes, namely priests, soldiers, herdsmen, swineherds, tradesmen, interpreters, and steersmen; and Megasthenês may therefore have taken it for granted that there were seven castes in India. It is a curious fact that, from the time of Alexander's expedition to a comparatively recent date, geographers and others have continually drawn analogies between Egypt and India."—Wheeler's *Hist. of India*, vol. III. p. 192, note [54-56]. Conf. Fragm. xxxvi.

† For some remarks on this point see Blochmann's translation of the *Aîn-i-Akbarî*, p. 118.

also decide cases in which foreigners are concerned, with the greatest care, and come down sharply on those who take unfair advantage of them. [What we have now said regarding India and its antiquities will suffice for our present purpose.]

BOOK I.

FRAGM. II.

Arr. *Exped. Alex.* V. 6. 2-11.

Of the Boundaries of India, its General Character, and its Rivers.‡

According to Eratosthenês, and Megasthenês who lived with Sibурtios the satrap of Arachôsia, and who, as he himself tells us, often visited Sandrakottos§ the king of the Indians, India forms the largest of the four parts into which Southern Asia is divided, while the smallest part is that region which is included between the Euphrates and our own sea. The two remaining parts, which are separated from the others by the Euphrates and the Indus, and lie between these rivers, are scarcely of sufficient size to be compared with India, even should they be taken both together. The same writers say that India is bounded on its

‡ Conf. Epit. *ad init.*

§ The name of Chandragupta is written by the Greeks Sandrokottos, Sandrakottas, Sandrakottos, Androkottos, and (best) Sandrokuptos. Cf. Schlegel, *Bibl. Ind.* I. 245.—Schwanbeck, p. 12, n. 6.

eastern side, right onwards to the south, by the great ocean; that its northern frontier is formed by the Kaukasos range as far as the junction of that range with Tauros; and that the boundary towards the west and the north-west, as far as the great ocean, is formed by the river Indus. A considerable portion of India consists of a level plain, and this, as they conjecture, has been formed from the alluvial deposits of the river,—inferring this from the fact that in other countries plains which are far away from the sea are generally formations of their respective rivers, so that in old times a country was even called by the name of its river. As an instance, there is the so-called plain of the Hermos—a river in Asia (Minor), which, flowing from the Mount of Mother Dindymênê, falls into the sea near the Æolian city of Smyrna. There is also the Lydian plain of the Kaüstros, named after that Lydian river; and another, that of the Kaïkos, in Mysia; and one also in Karia,—that of the Maiandros, which extends even to Miletos, which is an Ionian city. [As for Egypt, both the historians Herodotus and Hekataios (or at any rate the author of the work on Egypt if he was other than Hekataios) alike agree in declaring it to be the gift of the Nile, so that that country was perhaps even called after the river; for in early times Aigyptos was the name of the river which now-a-days both the Egyptians and other nations call the Nile, as the words of Homer clearly prove, when he says that Menelaös stationed his ships at the mouth of the river Aigyptos. If, then, there is but a single river in each plain, and these rivers, though by no means large, are capable of forming, as they flow to the sea, much new land, by carrying down silt from the uplands, where their sources are, it would be unreasonable to reject the belief in the case of India that a great part of it is a level plain, and that this plain is formed from the silt deposited by the rivers, seeing that the Hermos, and the Kaüstros, and the Kaïkos, and the Maiandros, and all the many rivers of Asia which fall into the Mediterranean, even if united, would not be fit to be compared in volume of water with an ordinary Indian river, and much less with the greatest of them all, the Ganges, with which neither the Egyptian Nile, nor the Danube which flows through Europe, can for a moment be compared. Nay, the whole of these if combined all into one are not equal even to the Indus, which is already a large river where it rises from its fountains, and which after receiving as tributaries fifteen rivers all greater than those of Asia, and bearing off from its rival the honour of giving name to the country, falls at last into the sea.*

---

* *Strabo*, XV. 1. 32, p. 700.—[All the rivers mentioned (the last of which is the Hupanis) unite in one, the Indus.] They say that fifteen considerable rivers, in all, flow into it.

Fragm. III.

Arr. *Indica*, II. 1. 7.

Of the Boundaries of India.†

(See translation of Arrian.)

Fragm. IV.

Strabo, XV. i. 11,—p. 689.

Of the Boundaries and Extent of India.‡

India is bounded on the north by the extremities of Tauros, and from Ariana to the

† Conf. Epit. 1, and for notes on the same see *Indian Antiquary*, vol. V. p. 330.—Ed.

‡ Conf. Epit. 1, 2. Pliny (*Hist. Nat.* VI. 21. 2) states that India extends from north to south 28,150 thousand paces. This number, though it is not exactly equal to 22,300 stadia, but to 22,800, nevertheless approaches the number given by Megasthenês nearer than any other. From the numbers which both Arrian (*Ind.* iii. 8) and Strabo (pp. 68-69, 690) give, Diodorus differs remarkably, for he says the breadth extends to 28,000, and the length to 32,000 stadia. It would be rash to deny that Megasthenês may also have indicated the larger numbers of Diodorus, for Arrian (*Ind.* iii. 7-8) adds to the number the words "*where shortest*" and "*where narrowest;*" and Strabo (p. 689) has added to the expression of the breadth the words "*at the shortest,*" and, referring to Megasthenês and Dêimachos, says distinctly "*who state that in some places the distance from the southern sea is* 20,000 *stadia, and in others* 30,000 (pp. 68-69). There can be no doubt, however, that Megasthenês regarded the smaller, and Dêimachos the larger number as correct; for the larger seemed to Arrian unworthy of mention, and Strabo (p. 690) says decidedly, "*Megasthenês and Dêimachos incline to be more moderate in their estimate, for according to them the distance from the southern sea to Caucasus is over* 20,000 *stadia: Dêimachos, however, allows that the distance in some places exceeds* 30,000 *stadia*"! by which he quite excludes Megasthenês from this opinion. And at p. 72, where he mentions the 30,000 stadia of Dêimachos, he does not say a word of Megasthenês. But it must be certain that 16,000 stadia is the only measure Megasthenês gave of the breadth of India. For not only Strabo (p. 689)

Eastern Sea by the mountains which are variously called by the natives of these regions P a r a p a m i s o s, and H e m ô d o s, and H i m a o s,§ and other names, but by the Macedonians K a u k a s o s.|| The boundary on the west is the river I n d u s, but the southern and eastern sides, which are both much greater than the others, run out into the Atlantic Ocean.¶ The shape of the country is thus rhomboïdal, since each of the greater sides exceeds its opposite side by 3000 stadia, which is the length of the promontory common to the south and the east coast, which projects equally in these two directions. [The length of the western side, measured from the Kaukasian mountains to the southern

---

and Arrian (*Ind.* iii. 7) have not quoted a larger number from Megasthenês, but Hipparchos also (Strabo, p. 69),—where he shows that Patroklês is unworthy of confidence, because he has given smaller dimensions for India than Megasthenês—only mentions the measure of 16,000 stadia; where, for what Hipparchos wanted, the greatest number was the most suitable for his proof.—I think the numbers were augmented because Megasthenês regarded as Indian, Kabul and that part of Ariana which Chandragupta had taken from Seleukos; and on the north the frontier nations Uttarakuras, which he mentions elsewhere. What Megasthenês said about the breadth of India remained fixed throughout the whole geography of the Greeks, so that not even Ptolemy, who says India extends 16,800 stadia, differs much from it. But his measure of length has either been rejected by all, for fear of opposing the ancient opinion that the torrid zone could not be inhabited, or (like Hipparchos) erroneously carried much too far to the north.—Schwanbeck, pp. 29, 30, n. 24.

§ Schmieder suggests Ἴμαος in Arrian.

|| *i.e.* The Himâlayas.

¶ The world was anciently regarded as an island surrounded by the Atlantic Sea.

sea along the course of the river Indus to its mouths, is said to be 13,000 stadia, so that the eastern side opposite, with the addition of the 3000 stadia of the promontory, will be somewhere about 16,000 stadia. This is the breadth of India where it is both smallest and greatest.] The length from west to east as far as Palibothra can be stated with greater certainty, for the royal road which leads to that city has been measured by *schoeni*, and is in length 10,000 stadia.* The extent of the parts beyond can only be conjectured from the time taken to make voyages from the sea to Palibothra by the Ganges, and may be about 6000 stadia. The entire length, computed at the shortest, will be 16,000 stadia. This is the estimate of Eratosthenês, who says he derived it principally from the authoritative register of the stages on the Royal Road. Herein Megasthenês agrees

---

* All the texts read *δισμυρίων* instead of *μυρίων*. In all the MSS. of Strabo also we read *σχοινίοις*, and in Arrian, who extracts the same passage from Megasthenês, everywhere *σχοίνοις*. Though there is nothing to blame in either lection, yet it is easier to change *σχοίνοις* than *σχοινίοις*, for Strabo may have been surprised to find the Greek *schoenus* in use also in India. The *schoenus*, however, which with Eratosthenês is a measure of 40 stadia (Plin. *Hist. Nat.* XII. 30), coincides precisely with the Indian *yôjana* of four *krôśas*. I do not forget that usually double this length is assigned to the *yôjana*, but also that it is shorter than the Hindus reckon it (*As. Res.* vol. V. p. 105), and also by the Chinese pilgrims (*Foe-koue-ki*, 87-88), and by Megasthenês himself, in Strabo (p. 708, Fragm. xxxiv. 3), from which it seems certain that ten stadia are equal to some Indian measure which cannot be a smaller one than the *krôśa*.—Schw. p. 27, n. 23.

with him. [Patroklês, however, makes the length less by 1000 stadia.] Conf. Arr. *Ind.* iii. 1-5.

Fragm. V.

Strabo, II. i. 7,—p. 69.

Of the Size of India.

Again, Hipparchos, in the 2nd volume of his commentary, charges Eratosthenês himself with throwing discredit on Patroklês for differing from Megasthenês about the length of India on its northern side, Megasthenês making it 16,000 stadia, and Patroklês 1000 less.

Fragm. VI.

Strabo, XV. i. 12,—pp. 689-690.

Of the Size of India.

[From this, one can readily see how the accounts of the other writers vary from one another. Thus Ktêsias says that India is not of less size than the rest of Asia; Onêsikritos regards it as the third part of the habitable world; and Nearchos says it takes one four months to traverse the plain only.] Megasthenês and Dêimachos incline to be more moderate in their estimate, for according to them the distance from the Southern Sea to Kaukasos is over 20,000 stadia.—[Dêimachos, however, allows that the distance in some places exceeds 30,000 stadia. Of these notice has been taken in an earlier part of the work.]

FRAGM. VII.

Strabo, II. i. 4,—pp. 68-69.

Of the Size of India.

Hipparchos controverts this view, urging the futility of the proofs on which it rests. Patroklês, he says, is unworthy of trust, opposed as he is by two competent authorities, Dêimachos and Megasthenês, who state that in some places the distance from the southern sea is 20,000 stadia, and in others 30,000. Such, he says, is the account they give, and it agrees with the ancient charts of the country.

FRAGM. VIII.

Arr. *Indica*, III. 7-8.

Of the Size of India.

With Megasthenês the breadth of India is its extent from east to west, though this is called by others its length. His account is that the breadth at shortest is 16,000 stadia, and its length—by which he means its extent from north to south—is at the narrowest 22,300 stadia.

FRAGM. IX.

Strabo, II. i. 19,—p. 76.

Of the setting of the Bear, and shadows falling in contrary directions.†

Again, he [Eratosthenês] wished to show the ignorance of Dêimachos, and his want of a

† Conf. Epit. 3.

practical knowledge of such subjects, evidenced as it was by his thinking that India lay between the autumnal equinox and the winter tropic, and by his contradicting the assertion of Megasthenês that in the southern parts of India the constellation of the Bear disappeared from view, and shadows fell in opposite directions,‡—phenomena which he assures us are never seen in India, thereby exhibiting the sheerest ignorance. He does not agree in this opinion, but accuses Dêimachos of ignorance for asserting that the Bears do nowhere in India disappear from sight, nor shadows fall in opposite directions, as Megasthenês supposed.

Fragm. X.

Pliny, *Hist. Nat.* VI. 22. 6.

Of the Setting of the Bear.

Next [to the Prasii] in the interior are the Monedes and the Suari, to whom belongs Mount Maleus, on which shadows fall towards the north in winter, and in summer to the south, for six months alternately.§ The Bears, Baeton

‡ Conf. Diod. II. 35, Plin. *Hist. Nat.* VI. 22. 6. The writers of Alexander's time who affirmed similar things were Nearchos and Onêsikritos, and Baeto who exceeded all bounds. Conf. Lassen, *Instit. Ling. Prac.* Append. p. 2. —Schwanb. p. 29.

§ "The Mandali would seem to be the same people as the Monedes of Pliny, who with the Suari, occupied the inland country to the south of the Palibothri. As this is the exact position of the country of the Mûndas and Suars, I think it quite certain that they must be the same race as the Monedes and Suari of Pliny. In another passage Pliny mentions the Mandei and Malli as occupying the country between the Calingæ and the Ganges. Amongst the Malli there was a mountain named Mallus, which

says, in that part of the country are only once visible in the course of the year, and not for more than fifteen days. Megasthenês says that this takes place in many parts of India.

Conf. Solin, 52. 13 :—

Beyond Palibothra is Mount Maleus, on which shadows fall in winter towards the north, and in summer towards the south, for six months alternately. The North Pole is visible in that part of the country once in the course of the year, and not for longer than fifteen days, as Baeton informs us, who allows that this occurs in many parts of India.

Fragm. XI.

Strabo, XV. i. 20,—p. 693.

Of the Fertility of India.‖

Megasthenês indicates the fertility of India by the fact of the soil producing two crops every year both of fruits and grain. [Eratosthenês writes to the same effect, for he speaks of a

---

would seem to be the same as the famous mount Maleus of the Monedes and Suari. I think it highly probable that both names may be intended for the celebrated mount Mandar, to the south of Bhâgulpur, which is fabled to have been used by the gods and demons at the churning of the ocean. The Mandei I would identify with the inhabitants of the Mahânadi river, which is the Manada of Ptolemy. The Malli or Malei would therefore be the same people as Ptolemy's Mandalæ, who occupied the right bank of the Ganges to the south of Palibothra, or they may be the people of the Rajmahâl hills who are called Maler . . . . The Suari of Pliny are the Sabarræ of Ptolemy, and both may be identified with the aboriginal Śavaras or Suars, a wild race of woodcutters who live in the jungles without any fixed habitation."—Cunningham's *Anc. Geog. of India*, pp. 508-9.

‖ Conf. Epit. 5, 9.

winter and a summer sowing, which both have rain: for a year, he says, is never found to be without rain at both those seasons, whence ensues a great abundance, since the soil is always productive. Much fruit is produced by trees; and the roots of plants, particularly of tall reeds, are sweet both by nature and by coction, since the moisture by which they are nourished is heated by the rays of the sun, whether it has fallen from the clouds or been drawn from the rivers. Eratosthenês uses here a peculiar expression: for what is called by others the ripening of fruits and the juices of plants is called among the Indians *coction*, which is as effective in producing a good flavour as the coction by fire itself. To the heat of the water the same writer ascribes the wonderful flexibility of the branches of trees, from which wheels are made, as also the fact of there being trees on which wool grows.¶]

Conf. Eratosth. *ap.* Strabo. XV. i. 13,—p. 690 :—

From the vapours arising from such vast rivers, and from the Etêsian winds, as Eratosthenês states, India is watered by the summer rains, and the plains are overflowed. During these rains, accordingly, flax* is sown and millet, also sesamum, rice, and *bosmorum*,† and in the winter time wheat, barley, pulse, and other esculent fruits unknown to us.

¶ Conf. Herod. II. 86. "*Velleraque ut foliis depectant tenuia Seres?*—Virgil, *Geor.* ii. 121.—Falconer.

* λίνον, perhaps the λίνον τὸ ἀπὸ δενδρέων of Arrian.

† βοσμορον—Strabo XV. i. 18.

FRAGM. XII.

Strabo, XV. i. 37,—p. 703.

Of some Wild Beasts of India.

According to Megasthenês the largest tigers are found among the Prasii, being nearly twice the size of the lion, and so strong that a tame tiger led by four men having seized a mule by the hinder leg overpowered it and dragged it to him. [2]The monkeys are larger than the largest dogs ; they are white except in the face, which is black, though the contrary is observed elsewhere. Their tails are more than two cubits in length. They are very tame, and not of a malicious disposition : so that they neither attack man nor steal. [3]Stones are dug up which are of the colour of frankincense, and sweeter than figs or honey. [4]In some parts of the country there are serpents two cubits long which have membranous wings like bats. They fly about by night, when they let fall drops of urine or sweat, which blister the skin of persons not on their guard, with putrid sores. There are also winged scorpions of an extraordinary size. [5]Ebony grows there. There are also dogs of great strength and courage, which will not let go their hold till water is poured into their nostrils : they bite so eagerly that the eyes of some become distorted, and the eyes of others fall out. Both a lion and a bull were held fast by a dog. The bull was seized by the muzzle, and died before the dog could be taken off.

FRAGM. XIII.‡

Ælian, *Hist. Anim.* XVII. 39. Conf. Fragm. XII. 2.

Of Indian Apes.

In the country of the Praxii,§ who are an Indian people, Megasthenês says there are apes not inferior in size to the largest dogs. They

‡ FRAGM. XIII. B.

Ælian, *Hist. Anim.* XVI. 10.

Of Indian Apes.

Among the Prasii in India there is found, they say, a species of apes of human-like intelligence, and which are to appearance about the size of Hurkanian dogs. Nature has furnished them with forelocks, which one ignorant of the reality would take to be artificial. Their chin, like that of a satyr, turns upward, and their tail is like the potent one of the lion. Their body is white all over except the face and the tip of the tail, which are of a reddish colour. They are very intelligent, and naturally tame. They are bred in the woods, where also they live, subsisting on the fruits which they find growing wild on the hills. They resort in great numbers to the suburbs of Latage, an Indian city, where they eat rice which has been laid down for them by the king's orders. In fact, every day a ready-prepared meal is set out for their use. It is said that when they have satisfied their appetite they retire in an orderly manner to their haunts in the woods, without injuring a single thing that comes in their way.

§ The *Prâchyas* (*i.e.* Easterns) are called by Strabo, Arrian, and Pliny Πράσιοι, *Prasii*; by Plutarch (*Alex.* 62) Πραίσιοι, a name often used by Ælian also; by Nikolaüs Damas. (ap. Stob. *Floril.* 37, 38) Πραύσιοι; by Diodorus (xvii. 93) Βρήσιοι; by Curtius (IX. 2, 3) *Pharrasii*; by Justin (xii. 8, 9) *Præsides*. Megasthenês attempted to approximate more closely to the Sanskrit *Prâchya*, for here he uses Πραξιακός. And it appears that Πράξιοι should be substituted for Πράσιοι in Stephan. Byzant., since it comes between the words Πράξιλος and Πρασ.—Schwanbeck, p. 82, not. 6.

have tails five cubits long, hair grows on their forehead, and they have luxuriant beards hanging down their breast. Their face is entirely white, and all the rest of the body black. They are tame and attached to man, and not malicious by nature like the apes of other countries.

FRAGM. XIV.

Ælian, *Hist. Anim.* XVI. 41. Conf. Fragm. XII. 4.

Of Winged Scorpions and Serpents.

Megasthenês says there are winged scorpions in India of enormous size, which sting Europeans and natives alike. There are also serpents which are likewise winged. These do not go abroad during the day, but by night, when they let fall urine, which if it lights upon any one's skin at once raises putrid sores thereon. Such is the statement of Megasthenês.

FRAGM. XV.

Strabo, XV. i. 56,—pp. 710-711.

Of the Beasts of India, and the Reed.

He (Megasthenês) says there are monkeys, rollers of rocks, which climb precipices whence they roll down stones upon their pursuers. [2]Most animals, he says, which are tame with us are wild in India, and he speaks of horses which are one-horned and have heads like those of deer; [3]and also of reeds some of which grow straight up to the height of thirty *orguiæ*,|| while

|| The *orguia* was four cubits, or equal to 6 feet 1 inch.

others grow along the ground to the length of fifty. They vary in thickness from three to six cubits in diameter.

FRAGM. XV.B.

Ælian, *Hist. Anim.* XVI. 20. 21. Conf. Fragm. XV. 2. 1.

Of some Beasts of India.

(20.) In certain districts of India (I speak of those which are most inland) they say there are inaccessible mountains infested by wild beasts, and which are also the haunts of animals like those of our own country except that they are wild; for even sheep, they say, run wild there, as well as dogs and goats and oxen, which roam about at their own pleasure, being independent and free from the dominion of the herdsman. That their number is beyond calculation is stated not only by writers on India, but also by the learned men of the country, among whom the Brachmans deserve to be reckoned, whose testimony is to the same effect. It is also said that there exists in India a one-horned animal, called by the natives the *Kartazôn*. It is of the size of a full-grown horse, and has a crest, and yellow hair soft as wool. It is furnished with very good legs and is very fleet. Its legs are jointless and formed like those of the elephant, and it has a tail like a swine's. A horn sprouts out from between its eyebrows, and this is not straight, but curved into the most natural wreaths, and is of a black colour. It is said to be extremely sharp, this horn. The animal, as I learn, has a voice beyond all example loud-ringing and dissonant. It allows other animals to approach it, and is good-natured *towards them*, though they say that with its congeners it is rather quarrelsome. The males are reported to have a natural propensity not only to fight among themselves, by butting with their horns, but to display a like animosity against the female, and to be so obstinate in their quarrels that they will not desist till a worsted rival is killed outright. But, again, not only is every member of the body of this animal endued with great strength, but such is the potency of its horn that nothing can withstand it. It loves to feed in secluded pastures, and wanders about alone, but at the rutting season it seeks the society of the female, and is then gentle towards her,—nay, the two even feed in company. The season being over and the female pregnant, the Indian *Kartazôn* again becomes ferocious and seeks solitude. The foals, it is said, are taken when quite young to the king of the Prasii, and are set to fight each other at the great public spectacles. No full-grown specimen is remembered to have ever been caught.

(21.) The traveller who crosses the mountains which skirt that frontier of India which is most inland meets, they say, with ravines which are clothed with very dense jungle, in a district called by the Indians Korouda.¶ These ravines are said to be the haunts of a peculiar kind of animal shaped like a satyr, covered all over with shaggy hair, and having a tail like a horse's, depending from its rump. If these creatures are left unmolested, they keep within the coppices, living on the wild fruits; but should they hear the hunter's

¶ V. L. Κόλουνδα.

halloo and the baying of the hounds they dart up the precipices with incredible speed, for they are habituated to climbing the mountains. They defend themselves by rolling down stones on their assailants, which often kill those they hit. The most difficult to catch are those which roll the stones. Some are said to have been brought, though with difficulty and after long intervals, to the Prasii, but these were either suffering from diseases or were females heavy with young, the former being too weak to escape, and the latter being impeded by the burden of the womb.—Conf. Plin. *Hist. Nat.* VII. 2. 17.

Fragm. XVI.

Pliny, *Hist. Nat.* VIII. 14. 1.

Of the Boa-Constrictor.

According to Megasthenês, serpents in India grow to such a size that they swallow stags and bulls whole.

Solinus, 52. 33.

So huge are the serpents that they swallow stags whole, and other animals of equal size.

Fragm. XVII.

Ælian, *Hist. Anim.* VIII. 7.

Of the Electric Eel.

I learn from Megasthenês that there is in the Indian Sea a small kind of fish which is never seen when alive, as it always swims in deep water, and only floats on the surface after it is dead. Should any one touch it he becomes faint and swoons,—nay, even dies at last.

FRAGM. XVIII.

Pliny, *Hist. Nat.* VI. 24. 1.

*Of Taprobane.**

Megasthenês says that Taprobane is separated *from the mainland* by a river; that the inhabitants are called Palaiogonoi,† and that their country is more productive of gold and large pearls than India.

Solin. 53. 3.

Taprobane is separated *from India* by a

---

* This island has been known by many names :—

1. Lanka.—The only name it goes by in Sanskṛit, and quite unknown to the Greeks and Romans.

2. Simundu or Palesimundu.—Probably a Greek form of the Sanskṛit *Pâli-Simanta*. This name had gone out of use before the time of Ptolemy the Geographer.

3. Taprobane.—Supposed to represent the Sanskṛit Tâmraparṇi ('red-leaved' or 'copper-coloured sand'), a slightly altered form of the Pâli Tambapaññî, which is found in the inscription of Aśoka on the Girnâr rock. Vide *ante*, vol. V. p. 272.

4. Salice (perhaps properly Saline), Serendivus, Sirlediba, Serendib, Zeilan, Ceylon. These are all considered to be derivatives from Siñala, the Pâli form of Siñhala, 'the abode of lions.' The affix *dib* represents the Sanskṛit *dvîpa*, 'an island.'

† Lassen has tried to account for the name Palaiogonoi thus (*Dissert. de insula Taprob.* p. 9) :—"We must suppose that Megasthenês was acquainted with the Indian myth that the first inhabitants of the island were said to have been Râkshasas or giants, the sons of the progenitors of the world, whom he might not inaptly call Palaiogonoi." Against this it may be remarked that, by this unusual term and so uncommon, Megasthenês meant to name the nation, not describe it; and next that Megasthenês is not in the habit of translating names, but of rendering them according to sound with some degree of paronomasia; lastly, that, shortly after, we find the name of Taprobane and of its capital Παλαισιμούνδος, quite like to Παλαιόγονοι. Accordingly as Lassen explains Παλαισιμούνδος, the name of the capital, by the Sanskrit *Pâli-simânta* ('head of the sacred doctrine'), I would also prefer to explain the name of the Palaiogonoi from the Sanskrit *Pâli-janâs* (*i.e.* 'men of the sacred doctrine').—Schwanbeck, p. 38, n. 35.

river flowing between: for one part of it abounds with wild beasts and elephants much larger than India breeds, and man claims the other part.

FRAGM. XIX.

Antigon. Caryst. 647.

Of Marine Trees.

Megasthenês, the author of the *Indika*, mentions that trees grow in the Indian Sea.

FRAGM. XX.

Arr. *Ind.* 4. 2-13.

Of the Indus and the Ganges.‡

See translation of Arrian.

FRAGM. XX.B.

Pliny. *Hist. Nat.* VI. 21. 9—22. 1.

The Prinas§ and the Cainas (a tributary of the Ganges) are both navigable rivers. The tribes which dwell by the Ganges are the Calingæ,|| nearest the sea, and higher up the Mandei, also the Malli, among whom is Mount Mallus, the boundary of all that region being the Ganges. Some have asserted that this river, like the Nile, rises from unknown sources, and in a similar way waters the country it flows through, while others trace its source to the Skythian mountains. Nineteen rivers are said to flow into it, of which, be-

‡ Conf. Epit. 15-19, and Notes on Arrian, *Ind. Ant.* vol. V. pp. 331, 332.

§ V. L. Pumas.

|| A great and widely diffused tribe settled mainly between the Mahânadî and the Godâvarî. Their capital was Partualis (called by Ptolemy Kalligra), on the Mahânadî, higher up than the site of Katak. The name is preserved in Koringa, a great port at the mouth of the Godâvarî.

sides those already mentioned, the Condochates,¶ Erannoboas, Cosoagus, and Sonus are navigable. According to other accounts, it bursts at once with thundering roar from its fountain, and tumbling down a steep and rocky channel lodges in a lake as soon as it reaches the level plain, whence it issues forth with a gentle current, being nowhere less than eight miles broad, while its mean breadth is a hundred stadia, and its least depth twenty fathoms.*

Solin. 52. 6-7.

In India the largest rivers are the Ganges and the Indus,—the Ganges, as some maintain, rising from uncertain sources, and, like the Nile,

---

¶ V. LL. Canucam, Vamam.

* "The Bhâgîratî (which we shall here regard as the true Ganges) first comes to light near Gangotrî, in the territory of Garhwâl, in lat. 30° 54′, long. 79° 7″, issuing from under a very low arch, at the base of a great snow-bed, estimated to be 300 feet thick, which lies between the lofty mountains termed St. Patrick, St. George, and the Pyramid, the two higher having elevations above the sea, respectively, of 22,798 and 22,654 feet, and the other, on the opposite side, having an elevation of 21,379. From the brow of this curious wall of snow, and immediately above the outlet of the stream, large and hoary icicles depend. They are formed by the freezing of the melted snow-water at the top of the bed; for in the middle of the day the sun is powerful, and the water produced by its action falls over this place in cascade, but is frozen at night . . . . At Sûkhî the river may be said to break though the 'Himâlaya Proper,' and the elevation of the waterway is here 7,608 feet. At Devprâg it is joined on the left side by the Alaknanda. . . . . From Devprâg the united stream is now called the Ganges . . . . . Its descent by the Dehra Dûn is rather rapid to Haṛidwâr . . . . sometimes called Gangâdwâra, or 'the gate of the Ganges,' being situate on its western or right bank at the southern base of the Sivâlik range, here intersected by a ravine or gorge by which the river, finally leaving the mountainous region, commences its course over the plains of Hindustân. The breadth of the river in the rainy season. . is represented to be a full mile."—*Thornton.*

overflowing its banks; while others think that it rises in the Skythian mountains. In India there is also the Hupanis,† a very noble river, which formed the limit of Alexander's march, as the altars set up on its banks testify. The least breadth of the Ganges is eight miles, and the greatest twenty. Its depth where least is fully one hundred feet.

Conf. Fragm. XXV. 1.

Some say that the least breadth is thirty stadia, but others only three; while Megasthenês says that the mean breadth is a hundred stadia, and its least depth twenty orguiæ.

FRAGM. XXI.

Arr. *Ind.* 6. 2-3.

Of the River Silas.‡

See translation of Arrian.

FRAGM. XXII.

Boissonade, *Anecd. Græc.* I. p. 419.

Of the River Silas.

There is in India a river called the Silas, named after the fountain from which it flows, on which nothing will float that is thrown into

† The same as the Huphasis or Satlej.

‡ Strab. 703, Diod. II. 37, and afterwards an anonymous writer whom Ruhnken (*ad Callimach. fragm.* p. 448) has praised, and whose account may be read in Boisson. *Anecd. Græc.* I. 419. The name is written Σίλλας in Diodorus, in Strabo Σιλίας, but best Σίλας, in the epitome of Strabo and in the *Anecd. Græc.* Bähr, 369, has collected the passages from Ktêsias. Lassen has also illustrated this fable (*Zeitschrift.* II. 63) from Indian literature:—"The Indians think that the river Silas is in the north, that it petrifies everything plunged in it, whence everything sinks and nothing swims." (Conf. *Mahâbhâr.* II. 1858.) Śilâ means 'a stone.'—Schw. p. 37, n. 32.

it, but everything sinks to the bottom, contrary to the usual law.

FRAGM. XXIII.

Strabo, XV. i. 38,—p. 703.

Of the River Silas.

(Megasthenês says) that in the mountainous country is a river, the S i l a s, on the waters of which nothing will float. Dêmokritos, who had travelled over a large part of Asia, disbelieves this, and so does Aristotle.

FRAGM. XXIV.

Arr. *Ind.* 5. 2.

Of the Number of Indian Rivers.

See translation of Arrian.

BOOK II.

FRAGM. XXV.

Strab. XV. i. 35. 36,—p. 702.

Of the city Pataliputra.§

According to Megasthenês the mean breadth (of the Ganges) is 100 stadia, and its least depth 20 fathoms. At the meeting of this river and another is situated Palibothra, a city eighty stadia in length and fifteen in breadth. It is of the shape of a parallelogram, and is girded with a wooden wall, pierced with loopholes for the discharge of arrows. It has a ditch in front for defence and for receiving the sewage of the city. The people in whose country this city is situated is the most distinguished in all India, and is called the Prasii. The king, in addition to his family

§ Conf. *Epit.* 36.

name, must adopt the surname of Palibothros, as Sandrakottos, for instance, did, to whom Megasthenês was sent on an embassy. [This custom also prevails among the Parthians, for all are called Arsakai, though each has his own peculiar name, as Orodês, Phraatês, or some other.]

Then follow these words:—

All the country beyond the Hupanis is allowed to be very fertile, but little is accurately known regarding it. Partly from ignorance and the remoteness of its situation, everything about it is exaggerated or represented as marvellous: for instance, there are the stories of the gold-digging ants, of animals and men of peculiar shapes, and possessing wonderful faculties; as the Sêres, who, they say, are so long-lived that they attain an age beyond that of two hundred years.|| They mention also an aristocratical form of government consisting of five thousand councillors, each of whom furnishes the state with an elephant.

According to Megasthenês the largest tigers are found in the country of the Prasii, &c. (Cf. Fragm. XII.)

Fragm. XXVI.

Arr. *Ind.* 10.

Of Pataliputra and the Manners of the Indians.

It is further said that the Indians do not rear monuments to the dead, but consider the

|| This was not the name of any particular nation, but was vaguely used to designate the inhabitants of the region producing silk, of which *Sêr* is the name in Chinese and in Japanese. The general opinion places this region (Sêrica) in Eastern Mongolia and the north-east of China, but it has also been sought for in Eastern Turkestân, in the Himâlaya towards the sources of the Ganges, in Assam, and even in Pegu. The name is first met with in Ktêsias.

virtues which men have displayed in life, and the songs in which their praises are celebrated, sufficient to preserve their memory after death. But of their cities it is said that the number is so great that it cannot be stated with precision, but that such cities as are situated on the banks of rivers or on the sea-coast are built of wood instead of brick, being meant to last only for a time,—so destructive are the heavy rains which pour down, and the rivers also when they overflow their banks and inundate the plains,—while those cities which stand on commanding situations and lofty eminences are built of brick and mud; that the greatest city in India is that which is called Palimbothra, in the dominions of the Prasians, where the streams of the Erannoboas and the Ganges unite,—the Ganges being the greatest of all rivers, and the Erannoboas being perhaps the third largest of Indian rivers, though greater than the greatest rivers elsewhere; but it is smaller than the Ganges where it falls into it. Megasthenês informs us that this city stretched in the inhabited quarters to an extreme length on each side of eighty stadia, and that its breadth was fifteen stadia, and that a ditch encompassed it all round, which was six hundred feet in breadth and thirty cubits in depth, and that the wall was crowned with 570 towers and had four-and-sixty gates. The same writer tells us further this remarkable fact about India, that all the

Indians are free, and not one of them is a slave. The Lakedæmonians and the Indians are here so far in agreement. The Lakedæmonians, however, hold the Helots as slaves, and these Helots do servile labour; but the Indians do not even use aliens as slaves, and much less a countryman of their own.

Fragm. XXVII.

Strab. XV. i. 53-56,—pp. 709-10.

Of the Manners of the Indians.

The Indians all live frugally, especially when in camp. They dislike a great undisciplined multitude, and consequently they observe good order. Theft is of very rare occurrence. Megasthenês says that those who were in the camp of Sandrakottos, wherein lay 400,000 men, found that the thefts reported on any one day did not exceed the value of two hundred drachmæ, and this among a people who have no written laws, but are ignorant of writing, and must therefore in all the business of life trust to memory. They live, nevertheless, happily enough, being simple in their manners and frugal. They never drink wine except at sacrifices.¶ Their beverage is a liquor composed from rice instead of barley, and their food is principally a rice-pottage.* The simplicity of their laws and their contracts is

¶ This wine was probably Soma juice.
* Curry and rice, no doubt.

proved by the fact that they seldom go to law. They have no suits about pledges or deposits, nor do they require either seals or witnesses, but make their deposits and confide in each other. Their houses and property they generally leave unguarded. These things indicate that they possess good, sober sense; but other things they do which one cannot approve: for instance, that they eat always alone, and that they have no fixed hours when meals are to be taken by all in common, but each one eats when he feels inclined. The contrary custom would be better for the ends of social and civil life.

Their favourite mode of exercising the body is by friction, applied in various ways, but especially by passing smooth ebony rollers over the skin. Their tombs are plain, and the mounds raised over the dead lowly. In contrast to the general simplicity of their style, they love finery and ornament. Their robes are worked in gold, and ornamented with precious stones, and they wear also flowered garments made of the finest muslin. Attendants walking behind hold up umbrellas over them: for they have a high regard for beauty, and avail themselves of every device to improve their looks. Truth and virtue they hold alike in esteem. Hence they accord no special privileges to the old unless they possess superior wisdom. They marry many wives, whom they buy from their parents, giving in exchange a yoke of oxen. Some they marry hoping to find in them willing helpmates; and others for pleasure and to fill their houses with children. The wives prostitute themselves unless they are compelled to be chaste. No one wears a crown at a sacrifice or libation, and they do not stab the victim, but strangle it, so that nothing mutilated, but only what is entire, may be presented to the deity.

A person convicted of bearing false witness suffers mutilation of his extremities. He who maims any one not only suffers in return the loss of the same limb, but his hand also is cut off. If he causes an artizan to lose his hand or his eye, he is put to death. The same writer says that none of the Indians employ slaves; [but Onesikritos says that this was peculiar to that part of the country over which Musikanos ruled.]†

The care of the king's person is entrusted to women, who also are bought from their parents.‡ The guards and the rest of the soldiery attend outside the gates. A woman who kills the king when drunk becomes the wife of his successor. The sons succeed the father. The king may not sleep during the daytime, and by night he is obliged to change his couch from

† His kingdom lay in Sindhu, along the banks of the Indus, and his capital was probably near Bakkar.

‡ This was not unknown in native courts of later times. Conf. Idrisi's account of the Balhara king.

time to time, with a view to defeat plots against his life.§

The king leaves his palace not only in time of war, but also for the purpose of judging causes. He then remains in court for the whole day, without allowing the business to be interrupted, even though the hour arrives when he must needs attend to his person,—that is, when he is to be rubbed with cylinders of wood. He continues hearing cases while the friction, which is performed by four attendants, is still proceeding. Another purpose for which he leaves his palace is to offer sacrifice; a third is to go to the chase, for which he departs in Bacchanalian fashion. Crowds of women surround him, and outside of this circle spearmen are ranged. The road is marked off with ropes, and it is death, for man and woman alike, to pass within the ropes. Men with drums and gongs lead the procession. The king hunts in the enclosures and shoots arrows from a platform. At his side stand two or three armed women. If he hunts in the open grounds he shoots from the back of an elephant. Of the women, some are in chariots, some on horses, and some even on elephants, and they are equipped with weapons

§ "The present king of Ava, who evidently belongs to the Indo-Chinese type, although he claims a Kshatriya origin, leads a life of seclusion very similar to that of Sandrokottos. He changes his bedroom every night, as a safeguard against sudden treachery." (Wheeler's *Hist. of India*, vol. III. p. 182, note.)

of every kind, as if they were going on a campaign.||

[These customs are very strange when compared with our own, but the following are still more so;] for Megasthenês states that the tribes inhabiting the Kaukasos have intercourse with women in public, and eat the bodies of their relatives,¶ and that there are monkeys which roll down stones, &c. (*Fragm. XV. follows, and then Fragm. XXIX.*)

Fragm. XXVII. B.

Ælian. *V. L.* iv. 1.

The Indians neither put out money at usury, nor know how to borrow. It is contrary to established usage for an Indian either to do or suffer a wrong, and therefore they neither make contracts nor require securities. Conf. Suid. *V.* Ἰνδοι.

Fragm. XXVII. C.

Nicol. Damasc. 44; Stob. *Serm.* 42.

Among the Indians one who is unable to recover a loan or a deposit has no remedy at law. All the creditor can do is to blame himself *for trusting a rogue.*

Fragm. XXVII. D.

Nicol. Damasc. 44; Stob. *Serm.* 42.

He who causes an artisan to lose his eye or his hand is put to death. If one is guilty of a very heinous offence the king orders his hair to be

|| In the drama of *Sakuntalâ,* Râja Dushyanta is represented as attended in the chase by Yavana women, with bows in their hands, and wearing garlands of wild flowers.

¶ Herodotus (bk. iii. 38, 99, 101) has noted the existence of both practices among certain Indian tribes.

cropped, this being a punishment to the last degree infamous.

Fragm. XXVIII.

Athen. iv. p. 153.

Of the Suppers of the Indians.

Megasthenês, in the second book of his *Indika*, says that when the Indians are at supper a table is placed before each person, this being like a tripod. There is placed upon it a golden bowl, into which they first put rice, boiled as one would boil barley, and then they add many dainties prepared according to Indian receipts.

Fragm. XXIX.*

Strab. XV. i. 57,—p. 711.

Of fabulous tribes.

But deviating into fables he says there are men five spans and even three spans in height, some of whom want the nose, having only two orifices above the mouth through which they breathe. * Against the men of three spans, war, as Homer has sung, is waged by the cranes, and also by partridges, which are as large as geese.†

---

* Cf. Strab. II. i. 9,—p. 70:—Dêimachos and Megasthenês are especially unworthy of credit. It is they who tell those stories about the men who sleep in their ears, the men without mouths, the men without nostrils, the men with one eye, the men with long legs, and the men with their toes turned backward. They renewed Homer's fable about the battle between the Cranes and the Pygmies, asserting that the latter were three spans in height. They told of the ants that dig for gold, of Pans with wedge-shaped heads, and of serpents swallowing down oxen and stags, horns and all,—the one author meanwhile accusing the other of falsehood, as Eratosthenês has remarked.

† Ktêsias in his *Indika* mentions Pygmies as belonging to India. The Indians themselves considered them as belonging to the race of the Kirâtæ, a barbarous people who inhabited woods and mountains and lived by hunting, and who were so diminutive that their name became a synonym

These people collect and destroy the eggs of the cranes, for it is in their country the cranes lay their eggs, and thus the eggs and the young cranes are not to be found anywhere else. Frequently a crane escapes having the brazen point of a weapon *in its body*, from wounds received in that country. [8] Equally absurd is the account given of the Enô-tokoitai,‡

---

for dwarf. They were thought to fight with vultures and eagles. As they were of Mongolian origin, the Indians represented them with the distinctive features of that race, but with their repulsiveness exaggerated. Hence Megasthenês spoke of the Amuktêres, men without noses, who had merely breathing-holes above the mouth. The Kirâtæ are no doubt identical with the Scyrites (V. L. Syrictes) of Plinius and the Kirrhadai of the *Periplus Maris Erythræi*.

‡ The Enôtokoitai are called in Sanskrit *Karṇaprâvaramâs*, and are frequently referred to in the great epic poems—*e.g.* *Mahâbh.* II. 1170, 1875. The opinion was universally prevalent among the Indians that barbarous tribes had large ears: thus not only are the *Karṇaprâvaramâs* mentioned, but also *Karṇikâs*, *Lambakarṇâs*, *Mahâkarṇâs* (*i.e.* long or large eared), *Ushṭrakarṇâs* (*i.e.* camel-eared), *Oshṭhakarṇâs* (*i.e.* having the ears close to the lips), *Pâṇikarṇâs* (*i.e.* having hands for ears). Schwanb. 66. "It is easy," says Wheeler (*Hist. Ind.* vol. III. p. 179), "for any one conversant with India to point out the origin of many of the so-called fables. The ants are not as big as foxes, but they are very extraordinary excavators. The stories of men pulling up trees, and using them as clubs, are common enough in the *Mahâbhârata*, especially in the legends of the exploits of Bhîma. Men do not have ears hanging down to their feet, but both men and women will occasionally elongate their ears after a very extraordinary fashion by thrusting articles through the lobe. . . . . If there was one story more than another which excited the wrath of Strabo, it was that of a people whose ears hung down to their feet. Yet the story is still current in Hindustân. Bâbu Johari Dâs says:—'An old woman once told me that her husband, a sepoy in the British army, had seen a people who slept on one ear, and covered themselves with the other.' (*Domestic Manners and Customs of the Hindus*, Banâras, 1860.)" The story may be referred to the Himâlayas. Fitch, who travelled

of the wild men, and of other monsters. [4] The wild men could not be brought to Sandrakottos, for they refused to take food and died. Their heels are in front, and the instep and toes are turned backwards.§ [5] Some were brought *to the court* who had no mouths and were tame. They dwell near the sources of the Ganges, and subsist on the savour of roasted flesh and the perfumes of fruits and flowers, having instead of mouths orifices through which they breathe. They are distressed with things of evil smell, and [6] hence it is with difficulty they keep their hold on life, especially in a camp. Referring to the other monstrosities, the philosophers told him of the Okupedes, a people who in running could leave the horse behind;|| [7] of the Enotokoitai, who had ears reaching down to their feet, so that they could sleep in them, and were so strong that they could pull up trees and break a bowstring. [8] Of others the Monommatoi, who have the

---

in India about 1585, says that a people in Bhutân had ears a span long."

§ These wild men are mentioned both by Ktêsias and Baeto. They were called Antipodes on account of the peculiar structure of their foot, and were reckoned among Æthiopian races, though they are often referred to in the Indian epics under the name *Paśchâdangulajas,* of which the ὀπισθοδάκτυλοι of Megasthenês is an exact translation. *Vide* Schwanb. 68.

|| 'Okupedes' is a transliteration into Greek, with a slight change, of the Sanskrit *Êkapadas,* ('having one foot'), the name of a tribe of the Kirâtæ noted for swiftness of foot, the quality indicated by the Greek term. The Monopodes are mentioned by Ktêsias, who confounded them with the Skiapodes, the men who covered themselves with the shadow of their foot.

ears of a dog, their one eye set in the middle of their forehead, the hair standing erect, and their breasts shaggy; ¶ of the Amuktêres also, a people without nostrils, who devour everything, eat raw meat, and are short-lived, and die before old age supervenes.* The upper part of the mouth protrudes far over the lower lip. [9] With regard to the Hyperboreans, who live a thousand years, they give the same account as Simonidês, Pindaros, and other mythological writers.† [10] The story told by Timagenês, that

---

¶ What Megasthenês here mentions as the characteristics of a single tribe are by the Indians attributed to several. The one-eyed men they are wont to call *êkâkshâs* or *ekavilo-chanâs*—the men with hair standing erect, *urdhvakeśa.* Indian *Cyclôpes* even are mentioned under the name of *Lalâṭâkshas, i.e.* having one eye in the forehead: *vide* Schwanb. 70.

* "That the *Astomi* are mentioned in the Indian books we cannot show so well as in the case of the Amuktêres, whom Megasthenês describes as *παμφάγους, ὠμοφάγους, 'ολιγοχρονιόυς.* Nevertheless the very words of the description are a proof that he followed the narratives of the Indians, for the words Παμφάγος, &c. by which he has described the Amuktêres, are very rarely used in Greek, and are translations of Indian words." Schwanb. 69.

† Pindar, who locates the Hyperboreans somewhere about the mouths of the Ister, thus sings of them:—

"But who with venturous course through wave or waste
To Hyperborean haunts and wilds untraced;
E'er found his wondrous way?
There Perseus pressed amain,
And 'midst the feast entered their strange abode,
Where hecatombs of asses slain
To soothe the radiant god
Astounded he beheld. Their rude solemnities,
Their barbarous shouts, Apollo's heart delight:
Laughing the rampant brute he sees
Insult the solemn rite.
Still their sights, their customs strange,
Scare not the 'Muse,' while all around

showers fall of drops of copper, which are swept together, is a fable. [11] Megasthenês states—what is more open to belief, since the same is

---

The dancing virgins range,
  And melting lyres and piercing pipes resound.
With braids of golden bays entwined
Their soft resplendent locks they bind,
  And feast in bliss the genial hour:
Nor foul disease, nor wasting age,
Visit the sacred race; nor wars they wage,
  Nor toil for wealth or power."

(10th Pythian ode, ll. 46 to 69, A. Moore's metrical version.)

Megasthenês had the penetration to perceive that the Greek fable of the Hyperboreans had an Indian source in the fables regarding the *Uttarakurus*. This word means literally the 'Kuru of the North.' "The historic origin," says P. V. de Saint-Martin, "of the Sanskrit appellation *Uttarakuru* is unknown, but its acceptation never varies. In all the documents of Upavedic literature, in the great poems, in the Purâṇas,—wherever, in short, the word is found,—it pertains to the domain of poetic and mythological geography. Uttarakuru is situated in the uttermost regions of the north at the foot of the mountains which surround Mount Mêru, far beyond the habitable world. It is the abode of demigods and holy Rishis whose lives extend to several thousands of years. All access to it is forbidden to mortals. Like the Hyperborean region of Western mythologists, this too enjoys the happy privilege of an eternal spring, equally exempt from excess of cold and excess of heat, and there the sorrows of the soul and the pains of the body are alike unknown. . . . . It is clear enough that this land of the blest is not of our world.

"In their intercourse with the Indians after the expedition of Alexander, the Greeks became acquainted with these fictions of Brâhmaṇic poetry, as well as with a good many other stories which made them look upon India as a land of prodigies. Megasthenês, like Ktêsias before him, had collected a great number of such stories, and either from his memoirs or from contemporary narratives, such as that of Dêimachos, the fable of the Uttarakurus had spread to the West, since, from what Pliny tells us (vi. 17, p. 316) one Amômêtus had composed a treatise regarding them analogous to that of Hecatæus regarding the Hyperboreans. It is certainly from this treatise of Amômêtus that Pliny borrows the two lines which he devotes to his Attacoræ, 'that a girdle of mountains warmed with

the case in Iberia‡—that the rivers carry down gold dust, and that a part of this is paid by way of tribute to the king.

Fragm. XXX.

Plin. *Hist. Nat.* VII. ii. 14-22.

Of fabulous races.

According to Megasthenês, on a mountain called Nulo§ there live men whose feet are turned

---

the sun sheltered them from the blasts of noxious winds, and that they enjoyed, like the Hyperboreans, an eternal spring.' 'Gens hominum Attacorum, apricis ab omni noxio afflatu seclusa collibus, eadem, qua Hyperborei degunt, temperie.' (Plin. *loc. cit.* Ammianus Marcellinus, xxiii. 6, 64.) Wagner transfers this description to the Sêres in general, (of whom the *Attacoræ* of Pliny form part), and some modern critics (Mannert, vol. IV. p. 250, 1875; *Forbiger Handb. der alten Geogr.* vol. II. p. 472, 1844) have believed they could see in it a reference to the great wall of China.) We see from a host of examples besides this, that the poetic fables and popular legends of India had taken, in passing into the Greek narratives, an appearance of reality, and a sort of historical consistency." (*E'tude sur la Géographie Grecque et Latine de l'Inde*, pp. 413-414.) The same author (p. 412) says, "Among the peoples of Sêrica, Ptolemy reckons the *Ottorocorrhæ*, a name which in Pliny is written Attacoræ, and which Ammianus Marcellinus, who copies Ptolemy, distorts into Opurocarra. There is no difficulty in recognizing under this name the Uttarakuru of Sanskṛit books."

Schwanbeck (p. 70) quotes Lassen, who writes somewhat to the same effect:—"Uttarakuru is a part of Sêrica, and as the first accounts of India came to the West from the Sêres, perhaps a part of the description of the peaceful happy life of the Sêres is to be explained from the Indian stories of the Uttarakuru. The story of the long life of the Sêres may be similarly explained, especially when Megasthenês reckons the life attained by the Hyperboreans at 1000 years. The *Mahâbhârata* (VI. 264) says that the Uttarakurus live 1000 or 10,000 years. We conclude from this that Megasthenês also wrote of the Uttarakurus, and that he not improperly rendered their name by that of the Hyperboreans."—*Zeitschr.* II. 67.

‡ Not Spain, but the country between the Black Sea and the Caspian, now called Georgia.

§ V. L. Nullo.

backward, and who have eight toes on each foot; [a] while on many of the mountains there lives a race of men having heads like those of dogs, who are clothed with the skins of wild beasts, whose speech is barking, and who, being armed with claws, live by hunting and fowling.|| [[ab] Ktêsias asserts on his own authority that the number of these men was upwards of 120,000, and that there is a race in India whose females bear offspring but once in the course of their life, and that their children become at once grey-haired.]

. . . .

[a] Megasthenês speaks of a race of men among the Nomadic Indians who instead of nostrils have merely orifices, whose legs are contorted like snakes, and who are called Scyritæ. He speaks also of a race living on the very confines of India on the east, near the source of the Ganges, the Astomi, who have no mouth; who cover their body, which is all over hairy, with the soft down found upon the leaves of trees; and who live merely by breathing, and the perfume inhaled by the nostrils. They eat nothing, and they drink nothing. They require merely a variety of odours of roots and of flowers and of wild apples. The apples they carry with them when they go on a distant journey, that they may always have something to smell. Too strong an odour would readily kill them.

|| Called by Ktêsias Κυνοκέφαλοι, and in Sanskṛit *Śunamuchâs* or *Śvâmuchâs*.

[4] Beyond the Astomi, in the remotest part of the mountains, the Trispithami and the Pygmies are said to have their abode. They are each three spans in height—that is, not more than seven-and-twenty inches. Their climate is salubrious and they enjoy a perpetual spring, under shelter of a barrier of mountains which rise on the north. They are the same whom Homer mentions as being harassed by the attacks of the cranes. [5] The story about them is—that mounted on the backs of rams and goats, and equipped with arrows, they march down in spring-time all in a body to the sea, and destroy the eggs and the young of these birds. It takes them always three months to finish this yearly campaign, and were it not undertaken they could not defend themselves against the vast flocks of subsequent years. Their huts are made of clay and feathers and egg-shells. [Aristotle says that they live in caves, but otherwise he gives the same account of them as others.]. . . .

[[5b] From Ktêsias we learn that there is a people belonging to this race, which is called Pandorê and settled in the valleys, who live two hundred years, having in youth hoary hair, which in old age turns black. On the other hand, others do not live beyond the age of forty,—nearly related to the Macrobii, whose women bear offspring but once. Agatharchidês says the same of them, adding that they subsist on locusts, and are swift of foot.] [6] Clitarchus and

Megasthenês call them M a n d i,¶ and reckon the number of their villages at three hundred. The females bear children at the age of seven, and are old women at forty.*

FRAGM. XXX.B.

Solin. 52. 26-30.

Near a mountain which is called Nulo there live men whose feet are turned backwards and have eight toes on each foot. Megasthenês writes that on different mountains in India there are tribes of men with dog-shaped heads, armed with claws, clothed with skins, who speak not in the accents of human language, but only bark, and have fierce grinning jaws. [In Ktêsias we read that in some parts the females bear offspring but once, and that the children are white-haired from their birth, &c.] . . . .

Those who live near the source of the Ganges, requiring nothing in the shape of food, subsist on the odour of wild apples, and when they go on a long journey they carry these with them for safety of their life, which they can support by inhaling their perfume. Should they inhale very foul air, death is inevitable.

FRAGM. XXXI.

Plutarch, *de facie in orbe lunæ*. (Opp. ed. Reisk, tom. ix. p. 701.)

Of the race of men without mouths.†

For how could one find growing there that

¶ Possibly we should read P â n d a i, unless perhaps Megasthenês referred to the inhabitants of Mount M a n d a r a.

* Conf. Fragm. L. 1, LI.

† Conf. Fragm. XXIX. 5, XXX. 3.

Indian root which Megasthenês says a race of men who neither eat nor drink, and in fact have not even mouths, set on fire and burn like incense, in order to sustain their existence with its odorous fumes, unless it received moisture from the moon?

BOOK III.

Fragm. XXXII.

Arr. *Ind.* XI. 1.-XII.-9. Cf. Epit. 40-53, and Plin. *Hist. Nat.* VI. xxii. 2, 3.

(See the translation of Arrian's *Indika.*)

Fragm. XXXIII.

Strab. XV. 1. 39-41, 46-49,—pp. 703-4, 707.

Of the Seven Castes among the Indians.

(39) According to him (Megasthenês) the population of India is divided into seven parts. The philosophers are first in rank, but form the smallest class in point of number. [a] Their services are employed privately by persons who wish to offer sacrifices or perform other sacred rites, and also publicly by the kings at what is called the Great Synod, wherein at the beginning of the new year all the philosophers are gathered together before the king at the gates, when any philosopher who may have committed any useful suggestion to writing, or observed any means for improving the crops and the cattle, or for promoting the public interests, declares it publicly. [a] If any one is detected giving false information thrice, the law condemns him to be silent for the rest of his life, but he who gives sound advice is exempted from paying any taxes or contributions.

(40) The *second* caste consists of the husbandmen, who form the bulk of the population, and are in disposition most mild and gentle. They are exempted from military service, and cultivate their lands undisturbed by fear. They never go to town, either to take part in its tumults, or for any other purpose. [5] It therefore not unfrequently happens that at the same time, and in the same part of the country, men may be seen drawn up in array of battle, and fighting at risk of their lives, while other men *close at hand* are ploughing and digging in *perfect* security, having these soldiers to protect them. The whole of the land is the property of the king, and the husbandmen till it on condition of receiving one-fourth of the produce.

(41) [6] The *third* caste consists of herdsmen and hunters, who alone are allowed to hunt, and to keep cattle, and to sell draught animals or let them out on hire. In return for clearing the land of wild beasts and fowls which devour the seeds sown in the fields, they receive an allowance of grain from the king. They lead a wandering life and live under tents.

Fragm. XXXVI. follows here.

[So much, then, on the subject of wild animals. We shall now return to Megasthenês, and resume from where we digressed.]

(46) [7] The *fourth* class, after herdsmen and hunters, consists of those who work at trades, of those who vend wares, and of those who are employed in bodily labour. Some of these pay tribute, and render to the state certain prescribed services. But the armour-makers and shipbuilders receive wages and their victuals from the king, for whom

alone they work. The general in command of the army supplies the soldiers with weapons, and the admiral of the fleet lets out ships on hire for the transport both of passengers and merchandize.

(47) The *fifth* class consists of f i g h t i n g m e n, who, when not engaged in active service, pass their time in idleness and drinking. They are maintained at the king's expense, and hence they are always ready, when occasion calls, to take the field, for they carry nothing of their own with them but their own bodies.

(48) The *sixth* class consists of the o v e r s e e r s, to whom is assigned the duty of watching all that goes on, and making reports secretly to the king. Some are entrusted with the inspection of the city, and others with that of the army. The former employ as their coadjutors the courtezans of the city, and the latter the courtezans of the camp. The ablest and most trustworthy men are appointed to fill these offices.

The *seventh* class consists of the c o u n c i l l o r s and a s s e s s o r s of the king. To them belong the highest posts of government, the tribunals of justice, and the general administration of public affairs.‡ [12] No one is allowed to marry out of his

‡ The Greek writers by confounding some distinctions occasioned by civil employment with those arising from that division have increased the number (of classes) from five (including the handicrafts-man or mixed class) to seven. This number is produced by their supposing the king's councillors and assessors to form a distinct class from the Brâhmans; by splitting the class of Vaisya into two, consisting of shepherds and husbandmen; by introducing a caste of spies; and by omitting the servile class altogether. With these exceptions the classes are in the state described by Menu, which is the groundwork of that still subsisting.—Elphinstone's *History of India*, p. 236.

own caste, or to exchange one profession or trade for another, or to follow more than one business. An exception is made in favour of the philosopher, who for his virtue is allowed this privilege.

Fragm. XXXIV.

Strab. XV. 1. 50-52,—pp. 707-709.

Of the administration of public affairs.

Of the use of Horses and Elephants.

(Fragm. XXXIII. has preceded this.)

(50) Of the great officers of state, some have charge of the market, others of the city, others of the soldiers. Some superintend the rivers, measure the land, as is done in Egypt, and inspect the sluices by which water is let out from the main canals into their branches, so that every one may have an equal supply of it. [2]The same persons have charge also of the huntsmen, and are entrusted with the power of rewarding or punishing them according to their deserts. They collect the taxes, and superintend the occupations connected with land, as those of the woodcutters, the carpenters, the blacksmiths, and the miners. [3]They construct roads, and at every ten stadia§ set up a pillar to show the by-roads and distances. [4]Those who have charge of the city are

§ From this it would appear that ten stadia were equal to some Indian measure of distance, which must have been the *krôśa* or *kosa*. If the stadium be taken at 202¼ yards, this would give 2022½ yards for the kos, agreeing with the shorter kos of 4,000 *hâths*, in use in the Panjâb, and till lately, if not still, in parts of Bengal.—Ed. *Ind. Ant.*

divided into six bodies of five each. The members of the first look after everything relating to the industrial arts. Those of the second attend to the entertainment of foreigners. To these they assign lodgings, and they keep watch over their modes of life by means of those persons whom they give to them for assistants. They escort them on the way when they leave the country, or, in the event of their dying, forward their property to their relatives. They take care of them when they are sick, and if they die bury them. [5]The third body consists of those who inquire when and how births and deaths occur, with the view not only of levying a tax, but also in order that births and deaths among both high and low may not escape the cognizance of Government. [6]The fourth class superintends trade and commerce. Its members have charge of weights and measures, and see that the products in their season are sold by public notice. No one is allowed to deal in more than one kind of commodity unless he pays a double tax. [7]The fifth class supervises manufactured articles, which they sell by public notice. What is new is sold separately from what is old, and there is a fine for mixing the two together. [8]The sixth and last class consists of those who collect the tenths of the prices of the articles sold. Fraud in the payment of this tax is punished with death.

[9]Such are the functions which these bodies

separately discharge. In their collective capacity they have charge both of their special departments, and also of matters affecting the general interest, as the keeping of public buildings in proper repair, the regulation of prices, the care of markets, harbours, and temples. [10]Next to the city magistrates there is a third governing body, which directs military affairs. This also consists of six divisions, with five members to each. One division is appointed to coöperate with the admiral of the fleet, another with the superintendent of the bullock-trains which are used for transporting engines of war, food for the soldiers, provender for the cattle, and other military requisites. They supply servants who beat the drum, and others who carry gongs; grooms also for the horses, and mechanists and their assistants. To the sound of the gong they send out foragers to bring in grass, and by a system of rewards and punishments ensure the work being done with despatch and safety. [11]The third division has charge of the foot-soldiers, the fourth of the horses, the fifth of the war-chariots, and the sixth of the elephants. [12]There are royal stables for the horses and elephants, and also a royal magazine for the arms, because the soldier has to return his arms to the magazine, and his horse and his elephant to the stables. [13]They use the elephants without bridles. The chariots are drawn on the march by oxen,[14] but the horses are led along by a halter, that their legs may not be galled and inflamed, nor their spirits damped by drawing chariots. [15]In addition to the charioteer, there are two fighting men who sit up in the chariot beside him. The war-elephant carries four men—three who shoot arrows, and the driver.|| (Fragm. XXVII. follows.)

FRAGM. XXXV.

Ælian, *Hist. Anim.* XIII. 10.

Of the use of Horses and Elephants.

Cf. Fragm. XXXIV. 13-15.

When it is said that an Indian by springing forward in front of a horse can check his speed and hold him back, this is not true of all Indians, but only of such as have been trained from boyhood to manage horses; for it is a practice with them to control their horses with bit and bridle, and to make them move at a measured pace and in a straight course. They neither, however, gall their tongue by the use of spiked muzzles, nor torture the roof of their mouth. The professional trainers break them in by forcing them to gallop round and round in a ring, especially when they see them refractory. Such as undertake this work require to have a strong hand as well as a thorough knowledge of

||"The fourfold division of the army (horse, foot, chariots, and elephants) was the same as that of Menu; but Strabo makes a sextuple division, by adding the commissariat and naval department."

horses. The greatest proficients test their skill by driving a chariot round and round in a ring; and in truth it would be no trifling feat to control with ease a team of four high-mettled steeds when whirling round in a circle. The chariot carries two men who sit beside the charioteer. The war-elephant, either in what is called the tower, or on his bare back in sooth, carries three fighting men, of whom two shoot from the side, while one shoots from behind. There is also a fourth man, who carries in his hand the goad wherewith he guides the animal, much in the same way as the pilot and captain of a ship direct its course with the helm.

Fragm. XXXVI.

Strab. XV. 1. 41-43,—pp. 704-705.

Of Elephants.

Conf. Epit. 54-56.

(Fragm. XXXIII. 6 has preceded this.)

A private person is not allowed to keep either a horse or an elephant. These animals are held to be the special property of the king, and persons are appointed to take care of them. [2] The manner of hunting the elephant is this. Round a bare patch of ground is dug a deep trench about five or six stadia in extent, and over this is thrown a very narrow bridge which gives access to the enclosure. [3] Into this enclosure are introduced three or four of the best-trained female elephants. The men themselves lie in ambush in concealed huts. [4] The wild elephants do not approach this trap in the daytime, but they enter it at night, going in one by one. [5] When all have passed the entrance, the men secretly close it up ; then, introducing the strongest of the tame fighting elephants, they fight it out with the wild ones, whom at the same time they enfeeble with hunger. [6] When the latter are now overcome with fatigue, the boldest of the drivers dismount unobserved, and each man creeps under his own elephant, and from this position creeps under the belly of the wild elephant and ties his feet together. [7] When this is done they incite the tame ones to beat those whose feet are tied till they fall to the ground. They then bind the wild ones and the tame ones together neck to neck with thongs of raw ox-hide. [8] To prevent them shaking themselves in order to throw off those who attempt to mount them, they make cuts all round their neck and then put thongs of leather into the incisions, so that the pain obliges them to submit to their fetters and to remain quiet. From the number caught they reject such as are too old or too young to be serviceable, and the rest they lead away to the stables. Here they tie their feet one to another, and fasten their necks to a firmly fixed pillar, and tame them by hunger. [10] After this they restore their strength with green reeds and grass. They next teach them to be obedient, which they effect by soothing them, some by *coaxing* words, and others by songs and the music of the drum. [11] Few of them are found difficult to tame, for they are naturally so mild and gentle in their disposition that they approximate to rational creatures. Some of them take up their drivers when fallen in battle, and carry them off in safety from the field. Others, when their masters have sought refuge between their forelegs, have fought in their defence and saved their lives. If in a fit of anger they kill either the man who feeds or the man who trains them, they pine so much for their loss that they refuse to take food, and sometimes die of hunger.

[12] They copulate like horses, and the female casts her calf chiefly in spring. It is the season for the male, when he is in heat and becomes ferocious. At this time he discharges a fatty substance through an orifice near the temples. It is also the season for the females, when the corresponding passage opens. [13] They go with young for a period which varies from sixteen to eighteen months. The dam suckles her calf for six years. [14] Most of them live as long as men who attain extreme longevity, and some live over two hundred years. They are liable to many distempers, and are not easily cured. [15] The remedy for diseases of the eye is to wash it with cows' milk. For most of their other diseases draughts of black wine are administered to them. For the cure of their wounds they are made to

swallow butter, for this draws out iron. Their sores are fomented with swine's flesh.

FRAGM. XXXVII.

Arr. *Ind.* ch. 13-14.

(Fragm. XXXII. comes before this.)

(See the translation of Arrian's *Indika.*)

[FRAGM. XXXVII. B.]

Ælian, *Hist. Anim.* XII. 44.

Of Elephants.

(Cf. Fragm. XXXVI. 9-10 and XXXVII. 9-10 *init.* c. XIV.).

In India an elephant if caught when full-grown is difficult to tame, and longing for freedom thirsts for blood. Should it be bound in chains, this exasperates it still more, and it will not submit to a master. The Indians, however, coax it with food, and seek to pacify it with various things for which it has a liking, their aim being to fill its stomach and to soothe its temper. But it is still angry with them, and takes no notice of them. To what device do they then resort? They sing to it their native melodies, and soothe it with the music of an instrument in common use *which has four strings* and is called a *skindapsos.* The creature now pricks up its ears, yields to the soothing strain, and its anger subsides. Then, though there is an occasional outburst of its suppressed passion, it gradually turns its eye to its food. It is then freed from its bonds, but does not seek to escape, being enthralled with the music. It even takes food eagerly, and, like a luxurious guest riveted to the festive board, has no wish to go, from its love of the music.

FRAGM. XXXVIII.

Ælian, *Hist. Anim.* XIII. 7.

Of the diseases of Elephants.

(Cf. Fragm. XXXVI. 15 and XXXVII. 15.)

The Indians cure the wounds of the elephants which they catch, in the manner following:—They treat them in the way in which, as good old

Homer tells us, Patroklos treated the wound of Eurypylos,—they foment them with lukewarm water.¶ After this they rub them over with butter, and if they are deep allay the inflammation by applying and inserting pieces of pork, hot but still retaining the blood. They cure ophthalmia with cows' milk, which is first used as a fomentation for the eye, and is then injected into it. The animals open their eyelids, and finding they can see better are delighted, and are sensible *of the benefit* like human beings. In proportion as their blindness diminishes their delight overflows, and this is a token that the disease has been cured. The remedy for other distempers to which they are liable is black wine; and if this potion fails to work a cure nothing else can save them.

Fragm. XXXIX.

Strab. XV. 1. 44,—p. 706.

*Of Gold-digging Ants.**

Megasthenês gives the following account of these ants. Among the Derdai, a great tribe of Indians, who inhabit the mountains on the

¶ See *Iliad*, bk. XI. 845.

* See *Ind. Ant.* vol. IV. pp. 225 *seqq.* where cogent arguments are adduced to prove that the 'gold-digging ants' were originally neither, as the ancients supposed, real ants, nor, as so many eminent men of learning have supposed, larger animals mistaken for ants on account of their appearance and subterranean habits, but Tibetan miners, whose mode of life and dress was in the remotest antiquity exactly what they are at the present day.

eastern borders,† there is an elevated plateau‡ about 3,000 stadia in circuit. Beneath the surface there are mines of gold, and here accordingly are found the ants which dig for that metal. They are not inferior in size to wild foxes. They run with amazing speed, and live by the produce of the chase. The time when they dig is winter.§ They throw up heaps of earth, as moles do, at the mouth of the mines. The gold-dust has to be subjected to a little boiling. The people of the neighbourhood, coming secretly with beasts of burden, carry this off. If they came openly the ants would attack them, and pursue them if they fled, and would destroy both them and their cattle. So, to effect the robbery without being observed, they lay down in several different places pieces of the flesh of wild beasts, and when the ants are by this device dispersed they carry off the gold-dust.

† These are the Dardæ of Pliny, the Daradrai of Ptolemy, and the Daradas of Sanskṛit literature. "The Dards are not an extinct race. According to the accounts of modern travellers, they consist of several wild and predatory tribes dwelling among the mountains on the north-west frontier of Kâśmîr and by the banks of the Indus." *Ind. Ant. loc. cit.*

‡ The table-land of Chojotol, see *Jour. R. Geog. Soc.* vol. XXXIX. pp. 149 *seqq.*—Ed. *Ind. Ant.*

§ "The miners of Thok-Jalung, in spite of the cold, prefer working in winter; and the number of their tents, which in summer amounts to three hundred, rises to nearly six hundred in winter. They prefer the winter, as the frozen soil then stands well, and is not likely to trouble them much by falling in."—*Id.*

This they sell to any trader they meet with|| while it is still in the state of ore, for the art of fusing metals is unknown to them.¶

FRAGM. XL.

Arr. *Ind.* XV.-5-7.

(See the translation of Arrian's *Indika.*)

[FRAGM. XL. B.]

Dio Chrysost. *Or.* 35,—p. 436, Morell.

Of Ants which dig for gold.

(Cf. Fragm. XXXIV. and XL.)

They get the gold from ants. These creatures are larger than foxes, but are in other respects like the ants of our own country. They dig holes in the earth like other ants. The heap which they throw up consists of gold the purest and brightest in all the world. The mounds are piled up close to each other in regular order like hillocks of gold dust, whereby all the plain is made effulgent. It is difficult, therefore, to look towards the sun, and many who have attempted to do this have thereby destroyed their eyesight. The people who are next neighbours to the ants, with a view to plunder these heaps, cross the intervening desert, which is of no great extent, mounted on wagons to which they have yoked their swiftest horses. They arrive at noon, a time when the ants have gone underground, and at

---

|| Τῳ τυχόντι τῶν ἐμπόρων. If the different reading τοῦ τυχόντος τοῖς ἐμπόροις be adopted, the rendering is, "*They dispose of it* to merchants at any price."

¶ Cf. Herod. III. 102-105; Arrian, *Anab.* V. 4. 7; Ælian, *Hist. Anim.* III. 4; Clem. Alex. *Pæd.* II. p. 207; Tzetz. *Chil.* XII. 330-340; Plin. *Hist. Nat.* XI. 36, XXXIII. 21; Propert. III. 13. 5; Pomp. Mel. VII. 2; Isidor. *Orig.* XII. 3; Albert Mag. *De Animal.* T. VI. p. 678, ex subdititiis Alexandri epistolis; Anonym. *De Monstris et Belluis*, 259, ed. Berger de Xivrey; Philostratus, *Vit. Apollon.* VI. 1; and Heliodorus, *Æth.* X. 26, p. 495; also Gildemeister, *Script. Arab. de reb. Ind.* p. 220-221, and 120; Busbequius, *Legationis Turcicæ Epist.* IV. pp. 144, or Thaunus XXIV. 7, p. 809.—Schwanbeck, p. 72.

once seizing the booty make off at full speed. The ants, on learning what has been done, pursue the fugitives, and overtaking them fight with them till they conquer or die, for of all animals they are the most courageous. It hence appears that they understand the worth of gold, and that they will sacrifice their lives rather than part with it.

Fragm. XLI.

Strab. XV. 1. 58-60,—pp. 711-714.

Of the Indian Philosophers.

(Fragm. XXIX. has preceded this.)

(58) Speaking of the philosophers, he (Megasthenês) says that such of them as live on the mountains are worshippers of Dionysos, showing as proofs *that he had come among them* the wild vine, which grows in their country only, and the ivy, and the laurel, and the myrtle, and the box-tree, and other evergreens, none of which are found beyond the Euphrates, except a few in parks, which it requires great care to preserve. They observe also certain customs which are Bacchanalian. Thus they dress in muslin, wear the turban, use perfumes, array themselves in garments dyed of bright colours; and their kings, when they appear in public, are preceded by the music of drums and gongs. But the philosophers who live on the plains worship Hêrakles. [These accounts are fabulous, and are impugned by many writers, especially what is said about the vine and wine. For the greater part of Armenia, and the whole of Mesopotamia and Media, onwards to Persia and Karmania, lie beyond the Eu-

phrates, and throughout a great part of each of these countries good vines grow, and good wine is produced.]

(59) Megasthenês makes a different division of the philosophers, saying that they are of two kinds—one of which he calls the Brachmanes, and the other the Sarmanes.* The Brachmanes are best esteemed, for they are more consistent in their opinions. From the time of their conception in the womb they are under the guardian care of learned men, who go to the mother and, under the pretence of using some incantations for the welfare of herself and her unborn babe, in reality give her prudent hints and counsels. The women who listen most willingly are thought to be the most fortunate in their children. After their birth the children are under the care of one person after another, and as

---

* "Since the word *Σαρμᾶνας* (the form used by Clemens of Alexandria) corresponds to the letter with the Sanskṛit word *Śramaṇa* (*i.e.* an ascetic), it is evident that the forms Γ*αρμᾶνας* and Γ*ερμᾶνας*, which are found in all the MSS. of Strabo, are incorrect. The mistake need not surprise us, since the ΣΑ when closely written together differ little in form from the syllable ΓΑ. In the same way Clement's Ἀ*λλόβιοι* must be changed into Strabo's Ὑ*λόβιοι*, corresponding with the Sanskṛit *Vanapṛastha*—'the man of the first three castes who, after the term of his householdership has expired, has entered the third *âśrama* or order, and has proceeded (*praśtha*) to a life in the woods (*Vâna*).'"—Schwanbeck, p. 46; H. H. Wilson, *Gloss.* "It is a capital question," he adds, "who the Sarmanæ were, some considering them to be Buddhists, and others denying them to be such. Weighty arguments are adduced on both sides, but the opinion of those seems to approach nearer the truth who contend that they were Buddhists."

they advance in age each succeeding master is more accomplished than his predecessor. The philosophers have their abode in a grove in front of the city within a moderate-sized enclosure. They live in a simple style, and lie on beds of rushes or (deer) skins. They abstain from animal food and sexual pleasures, and spend their time in listening to serious discourse, and in imparting their knowledge to such as will listen to them. The hearer is not allowed to speak, or even to cough, and much less to spit, and if he offends in any of these ways he is cast out from their society that very day, as being a man who is wanting in self-restraint. After living in this manner for seven-and-thirty years, each individual retires to his own property, where he lives for the rest of his days in ease and security.† They then array themselves in fine muslin, and wear a few trinkets of gold on their fingers and in their ears. They eat flesh, but not that of animals employed in labour. They abstain from hot and highly seasoned food. They marry as many wives as they please, with a view to have

† "A mistake (of the Greek writers) originates in their ignorance of the fourfold division of a Brâhmaṇ's life. Thus they speak of men who had been for many years sophists marrying and returning to common life (alluding probably to a student who, having completed the austerities of the first period, becomes a householder):" Elphinstone's *History of India*, p. 236, where it is also remarked that the writers erroneously prolong the period during which students listen to their instructors in silence and respect, making it extend in all cases to thirty-seven, which is the greatest age to which Manu (chap. III. sec. 1) permits it in any case to be protracted.

numerous children, for by having many wives greater advantages are enjoyed, and, since they have no slaves, they have more need to have children around them to attend to their wants.

The Brachmanes do not communicate a knowledge of philosophy to their wives, lest they should divulge any of the forbidden mysteries to the profane if they became depraved, or lest they should desert them if they became good philosophers: for no one who despises pleasure and pain, as well as life and death, wishes to be in subjection to another, but this is characteristic both of a good man and of a good woman.

Death is with them a very frequent subject of discourse. They regard this life as, so to speak, the time when the child within the womb becomes mature, and death as a birth into a real and happy life for the votaries of philosophy. On this account they undergo much discipline as a preparation for death. They consider nothing that befalls men to be either good or bad, to suppose otherwise being a dream-like illusion, else how could some be affected with sorrow, and others with pleasure, by the very same things, and how could the same things affect the same individuals at different times with these opposite emotions?

Their ideas about physical phenomena, the same author tells us, are very crude, for they are better in their actions than in their reasonings, inasmuch as their belief is in great measure based upon fables; yet on many points their opinions coincide with those of the Greeks, for like them they say that the world had a beginning, and is liable to destruction, and is in shape spherical, and that the Deity who made it, and who governs it, is diffused through all its parts. They hold that various first principles operate in the universe, and that water was the principle employed in the making of the world. In addition to the four elements there is a fifth agency, from which the heaven and the stars were produced.‡ The earth is placed in the centre of the universe. Concerning generation, and the nature of the soul, and many other subjects, they express views like those maintained by the Greeks. They wrap up their doctrines about immortality and future judgment, and kindred topics, in allegories, after the manner of Plato. Such are his statements regarding the Brachmanes.

(60) Of the Sarmanes§ he tells us that

‡ *Âkâśa*, 'the ether or sky.'

§ Schwanbeck argues from the distinct separation here made between the Brachmanes and the Sarmanes, as well as from the name *Śramaṇa* being especially applied to Bauddha teachers, that the latter are here meant. They are called Σαμαναῖοι by Bardesanes (ap. Porphyr. *Abstin.* IV. 17) and Alex. Polyhistor. (ap. *Cyrill. contra Julian.* IV. p. 133 E, ed. Paris, 1638). Conf. also Hieronym. *ad Jovinian.* II. (ed. Paris, 1706, T. II. pt. II. p. 206). And this is just the Pali name *Sammana*, the equivalent of the Sanskrit *Śramana*. Bohlen in *De Buddhaismi origine et ætate definiendis* sustains this view, but Lassen (*Rhein. Mus. für Phil.* I. 171 ff.) contends that the description agrees better with the Brâhmaṇ ascetics. See Schwanbeck, p. 45ff. and Lassen, *Ind. Alterth.* (2nd ed). II. 705, or (1st ed.) II. 700.

those who are held in most honour are called the Hylobioi.|| They live in the woods, where they subsist on leaves of trees and wild fruits, and wear garments made from the bark of trees. They abstain from sexual intercourse and from wine. They communicate with the kings, who consult them by messengers regarding the causes of things, and who through them worship and supplicate the deity. Next in honour to the Hylobioi are the physicians, since they are engaged in the study of the nature of man. They are simple in their habits, but do not live in the fields. Their food consists of rice and barley-meal, which they can always get for the mere asking, or receive from those who entertain them as guests in their houses. By their knowledge of pharmacy they can make marriages fruitful, and determine the sex of the offspring. They effect cures rather by regulating diet than by the use of medicines. The remedies most esteemed are ointments and plasters. All others they consider to be in a great measure pernicious in their nature.¶ This class and the other class practise fortitude, both by undergoing active toil, and by the endurance of pain, so that they remain for a whole day motionless in one fixed attitude.*

|| See note* page 98.

¶ "The habits of the physicians," Elphinstone remarks, "seem to correspond with those of Brâhmaṇs of the fourth stage."

* "It is indeed," says the same authority, "a remarkable

Besides these there are diviners and sorcerers, and adepts in the rites and customs relating to the dead, who go about begging both in villages and towns.

Even such of them as are of superior culture and refinement inculcate such superstitions regarding Hades as they consider favourable to piety and holiness of life. Women pursue philosophy with some of them, but abstain from sexual intercourse.

FRAGM. XLII.

Clem. Alex. *Strom.* I. p. 305 D (ed. Colon. 1688).

That the Jewish race is by far the oldest of all these, and that their philosophy, which has been committed to writing, preceded the philosophy of the Greeks, Philo the Pythagorean shows by many arguments, as does also Aristoboulos the Peripatetic, and many others whose names I need not waste time in enumerating. Megasthenês, the author of a work *on India*, who lived with Seleukos Nikator, writes most clearly on this point, and his words are these :—" *All that has been said regarding nature by the ancients is asserted also by philosophers out of Greece, on the one part in India by the Brachmanes, and on the other in Syria by the people called the Jews.*"

---

circumstance that the religion of Buddha should never have been expressly noticed by the Greek authors, though it had existed for two centuries before Alexander. The only explanation is that the appearance and manners of its followers were not so peculiar as to enable a foreigner to distinguish them from the mass of the people."

Fragm. XLII. B.

Euseb. *Præp. Ev.* IX. 6,—pp. 410 C, D (ed. Colon. 1688). *Ex* Clem. Alex.

Again, in addition to this, further on he writes thus :—

"Megasthenês, the writer who lived with Seleukos Nikator, writes most clearly on this point and to this effect :—'All that has been said,'" &c.

Fragm. XLII. C.

Cyrill. *Contra Julian.* IV. (Opp. ed. Paris, 1638, T. VI. p. 134 Al. *Ex* Clem. Alex.†

Aristoboulos the Peripatetic somewhere writes to this effect :—"All that has been said," &c.

Fragm. XLIII.

Clem. Alex. *Strom.* I. p. 305, A, B (ed. Colon. 1688).
Of the Philosophers of India.

[Philosophy, then, with all its blessed advantages to man, flourished long ages ago among the barbarians, diffusing its light among the Gentiles, and eventually penetrated into Greece. Its hierophants were the prophets among the Egyptians, the Chaldæans among the Assyrians, the Druids among the Gauls, the Sarmanæans who were the philosophers of the Baktrians and the Kelts, the Magi among the Persians, who, as you know, announced beforehand the birth of the Saviour, being led by a star till they arrived in the land of Judæa, and among the Indians the Gymnosophists, and other philosophers of barbarous nations.]

There are two sects of these Indian philosophers—one called the Sarmânai and the other the Brachmânai. Connected with the Sarmânai are the philosophers called the Hylobioi,‡ who

† "In this passage, though Cyril follows Clemens, he wrongly attributes the narrative of Megasthenês to Aristoboulos the Peripatetic, whom Clemens only praises."—Schwanbeck, p. 50.

‡ The reading of the MSS is Allobioi.

neither live in cities nor even in houses. They clothe themselves with the bark of trees, and subsist upon acorns, and drink water by lifting it to their mouth with their hands. They neither marry nor beget children [like those ascetics of our own day called the Enkratêtai. Among the Indians are those *philosophers* also who follow the precepts of B o u t t a,§ whom they honour as a god on account of his extraordinary sanctity.]

---

§ V. 1. Βούτα.—The passage admits of a different rendering: "They (the Hylobioi) are those among the Indians who follow the precepts of Boutta." Colebrooke in his *Observations on the Sect of the Jains*, has quoted this passage from Clemens to controvert the opinion that the religion and institutions of the orthodox Hindus are more modern than the doctrines of Jina and of Buddha. "Here," he says, "to my apprehension, the followers of Buddha are clearly distinguished from the Brachmanes and Sarmanes. The latter, called Germanes by Strabo, and Samanæans by Porphyrius, are the ascetics of a different religion, and may have belonged to the sect of Jina, or to another. The Brachmanes are apparently those who are described by Philostratus and Hierocles as worshipping the sun; and by Strabo and by Arrian as performing sacrifices for the common benefit of the nation, as well as for individuals ... They are expressly discriminated from the sect of Buddha by one ancient author, and from the Sarmanes (*a*) or Samanæans (ascetics of various tribes) by others. They are described by more than one authority as worshipping the sun, as performing sacrifices, and as denying the eternity of the world, and maintaining other tenets incompatible with the supposition that the sects of Buddha or Jina could be meant. Their manners and doctrine, as described by these authors, are quite conformable with the notions and practice of the orthodox Hindus. It may therefore be confidently inferred that the followers of the Vedas flourished in India when it was visited by the Greeks under Alexander, and continued to flourish from the time of Megasthenês, who described them in the fourth century before Christ, to that of Porphyrius, who speaks of them, on later authority, in the third century after Christ."

(*a*) *Samana* is the Pâli form of the older *Śramana*.

N

Fragm. XLIV.

Strab. XV. 1. 68,—p. 718.

Of Kalanos and Mandanis.

Megasthenês, however, says that self-destruction is not a dogma of the philosophers, but that such as commit the act are regarded as foolhardy, those naturally of a severe temper stabbing themselves or casting themselves down a precipice, those averse to pain drowning themselves, those capable of enduring pain strangling themselves, and those of ardent temperaments throwing themselves into the fire. Kalanos was a man of this stamp. He was ruled by his passions, and became a slave to the table of Alexander.‖ He is on this account condemned *by his countrymen*, but Mandanis is applauded because when messengers from Alexander invited him to go to the son of Zeus, with the promise of gifts if he complied, and threats of punishment if he refused, he did not go. Alexander, he said, was not the son of Zeus, for he was not so much as master of the larger half of the world. As for himself,

‖ "Kalanos followed the Makedonian army from Taxila, and when afterwards taken ill burnt himself on a funeral pyre in the presence of the whole Makedonian army, without evincing any symptom of pain. His real name, according to Plutarch, was Sphines, and he received the name Kalanos among the Greeks because in saluting persons he used the form καλέ instead of the Greek χαῖρε. What Plutarch here calls καλέ is probably the Sanskrit form *kalyâṇa*, which is commonly used in addressing a person, and signifies 'good, just, or distinguished.'"—Smith's *Classical Dictionary*.

he wanted none of the gifts of a man whose desires nothing could satiate; and as for his threats he feared them not: for if he lived, India would supply him with food enough, and if he died, he would be delivered from the body of flesh now afflicted with age, and would be translated to a better and a purer life. Alexander expressed admiration of the man, and let him have his own way.

FRAGM. XLV.

Arr. VII. ii. 3-9.

(See the translation of Arrian's *Indika*.)

BOOK IV.

FRAGM. XLVI.

Strab. XV. I. 6-8,—pp. 686-688.

That the Indians had never been attacked by others, nor had themselves attacked others.

(Cf. Epit. 23.)

6. But what just reliance can we place on the accounts of India from such expeditions as those of Kyros and Semiramis?¶ Megasthenês concurs in this view, and recommends his readers to put no

¶ "The expedition of Semiramis as described by Diodorus Siculus (II. 16-19), who followed the *Assyriaka* of Ktêsias, has almost the character of a legend abounding with puerilities, and is entirely destitute of those geographical details which stamp events with reality. If this expedition is real, as on other grounds we may believe it to be, some traces will assuredly be found of it in the cuneiform inscriptions of Nineveh, which are destined to throw so much unexpected light on the ancient history of Asia. It has already been believed possible to draw from these inscriptions the foundations of a positive chronology which will fully confirm the indications given by Herodotus as

faith in the ancient history of India. Its people, he says, never sent an expedition abroad, nor was their country ever invaded and conquered except by Hêrakles and Dionysos *in old times*, and by the Makedonians in our own. Yet Sesôstris the Egyptian* and Tearkôn the Ethiopian ad-

---

to the epoch of Semiramis, in fixing the epoch of this celebrated queen in the 8th century of our era—an epoch which is quite in harmony with the *data* which we possess from other sources regarding the condition of the North-West of India after the Vedic times.

"Kyros, towards the middle of the 6th century of our era, must also have carried his arms even to the Indus. Historical tradition attributed to him the destruction of Kapisa, an important city in the upper region of the Kôphês (Plin. VI. 23); and in the lower region the Assakenians and the Astakenians, indigenous tribes of Gandara, are reckoned among his tributaries (Arrian, *Indika*, I. 3). Tradition further recounted that, in returning from his expedition into India, Kyros had seen his whole army perish in the deserts of Gedrosia (Arr. *Anab.* VI. 24. 2). The Persian domination in these districts has left more than one trace in the geographical nomenclature. It is sufficient to recall the name of the Khoaspês, one of the great affluents of the Kôphês.

"Whatever be the real historical character of the expeditions of Semiramis and Kyros, it is certain that their conquests on the Indus were only temporary acquisitions, since at the epoch when Dareios Hystaspês mounted the throne the eastern frontier of the empire did not go beyond Arakhosia (the *Haraqaiti* of the Zend texts, the *Haraouvatis* of the cuneiform inscriptions, the *Arrokhadj* of Musalmân geography, the provinces of *Kandahâr* and of *Ghazni* of existing geography)—that is to say, the parts of Afghânistân which lie east of the Sulimân chain of mountains. This fact is established by the great trilingual inscription of Bisoutoun, which indicates the last eastern countries to which Dareios had carried his arms at the epoch when the monument was erected. This was before he had achieved his well-known conquest of the valley of the Indus."—St. Martin, *E'tude sur la GéographieGrecque et Latine de l'Inde*, pp. 14 *seqq*.

* Sesostris (called Sesoôsis by Diodorus) has generally been identified with Ramses the third king of the 19th dynasty of Manetho, the son of Seti, and the father of

vanced as far as Europe. And Nabukodrosor,† who is more renowned among the Chaldæans than even Hêrakles among the Greeks, carried his arms to the Pillars,‡ which Tearkôn also reached, while Sesôstris penetrated from Ibêria even into Thrace and Pontos. Besides these there was Idanthyrsos the Skythian, who overran Asia as far as Egypt.§ But not one of these great conquerors approached India, and Semiramis, who meditated its conquest, died before the necessary preparations were undertaken. The Persians indeed summoned the Hydrakai‖ from India to serve as mercenaries, but they did not lead an army into the country, and only approached its borders when Kyros marched against the Massagetai.

Of Dionysos and Hêrakles.

7. The accounts about Hêrakles and

Menephthah the Pharaoh of the Exodus. Lepsius, however, from a study of the Tablet of Rameses II. found at Abydos in Egypt, and now in the British Museum, has been led to identify him with the Sesortasen or Osirtasen of the great 12th dynasty.—See *Report of the Proceedings of the Second International Congress of Orientalists*, p. 44.

† V. l. Ναβοκοδρόσορον.

‡ Called by Ptolemy the "Pillars of Alexander," above Albania and Iberia at the commencement of the Asiatic Sarmatia.

§ Herodotus mentions an invasion of Skythians which was led by Madyas. As Idanthyrsos may have been a common appellative of the Skythian kings, Strabo may here be referring to that invasion.

‖ The Hydrakai are called also Oxydrakai. The name, according to Lassen, represents the Sanskrit *Kshudraka*. It is variously written Sydrakai, Syrakusai, Sabagræ, and Sygambri.

D i o n y s o s, Megasthenês and some few authors with him consider entitled to credit, [but the majority, among whom is Eratosthenês, consider them incredible and fabulous, like the stories current among the Greeks.......]

8. On such grounds they called a particular race of people Nyssaians, and their city N y s s a,¶ which Dionysos had founded, and the mountain which rose above the city M ê r o n, assigning as their reason for bestowing these names that ivy grows there, and also the vine, although its fruit does not come to perfection, as the clusters, on account of the heaviness of the rains, fall off the trees before ripening. They further called the O x y d r a k a i descendants of Dionysos, because the vine grew in their country, and their processions were conducted with great pomp, and their kings on going forth to war and on other occasions marched in Bacchic fashion, with drums beating, while they were dressed in gay-coloured robes, which is also a custom among other Indians. Again, when Alexander had captured at the first assault the rock called A o r n o s, the base of which is washed by the Indus near its source, his followers, magnifying the affair, affirmed that Hêrakles had thrice assaulted the same rock and had been thrice repulsed.* They

¶ V. ll. Νυσαίους, Νύσαν.

* This celebrated rock has been identified by General Cunningham with the ruined fortress of R â ṇ î g a t, situated immediately above the small village of Nogrâm, which lies about sixteen miles north by west from

said also that the S i b a e were descended from those who accompanied Hêrakles on his expedition, and that they preserved badges of their descent, for they wore skins like Hêrakles, and carried clubs, and branded the mark of a cudgel on their oxen and mules.† In support of this story they turn to account the legends regarding Kaukasos and Promêtheus by transferring them hither from Pontos, which they did on the slight pretext that they had seen a sacred cave among the P a r o p a m i s a d a e. This they declared was the prison of Promêtheus, whither Hêrakles had come to effect his deliverance, and that this was the Kaukasos, to which the Greeks represent Promêtheus as having been bound.‡

O h i n d, which he takes to be the Embolima of the ancients. "Râṇîgat," he says, "or the Queen's rock, is a large upright block on the north edge of the fort, on which Râja V a r a's *rânî* is said to have seated herself daily. The fort itself is attributed to Râja Vara, and some ruins at the foot of the hill are called Râja Vara's stables . . . I think, therefore, that the hill-fort of Aornos most probably derived its name from Râja Vara, and that the ruined fortress of R â ṇ î g a t has a better claim to be identified with the Aornos of Alexander than either the Mahâban hill of General Abbott, or the castle of Râja Hodi proposed by General Court and Mr. Loewenthal." See Grote's *History of India*, vol. VIII. pp. 437-8, footnote.

† According to Curtius, the Sibae, whom he calls Sobii, occupied the country between the Hydaspês and the Akesinês. They may have derived their name from the god Śiva.

‡ "No writer before Alexander's time mentions the Indian gods. The Makedonians, when they came into India, in accordance with the invariable practice of the Greeks, considered the gods of the country to be the same as their own. Śiva they were led to identify with Bacchus on their observing the unbridled license and somewhat Bacchic fashion of his worship, and because they traced

Fragm. XLVII.

Arr. *Ind.* V. 4-12.

(See the translation of Arrian's *Indika.*)

Fragm. XLVIII.

Josephus *Contra Apion.* I. 20 (T. II. p. 451, Haverc.).

Of Nabuchodrosor.

(Cf. Fragm. XLVI. 2.)

Megasthenês also expresses the same opinion *in the 4th book of his Indika*, where he endeavours to show that the aforesaid king of the Babylonians (Nabouchodonosor) surpassed Hêrakles in courage and the greatness of his achievements, by telling us that he conquered even Ibêria.

Fragm. XLVIII. B.

Joseph. *Ant. Jud.* X. ii. 1 (T. I. p. 538, Haverc.).

[In this place (Nabouchodonosor) erected also of stone elevated places for walking about on,

---

some slight resemblance between the attributes of the two deities, and between the names belonging to the mythic conception of each. Nor was anything easier, after Euripides had originated the fiction that Dionysos had roamed over the East, than to suppose that the god of luxuriant fecundity had made his way to India, a country so remarkable for its fertility. To confirm this opinion they made use of a slight and accidental agreement in names. Thus Mount Mêru seemed an indication of the god who sprang from the thigh of Zeus (ἐκ διὸς μήρου). Thus they thought the Kydrakæ (Oxydrukai) the offspring of Dionysos because the vine grew in their country, and they saw that their kings displayed great pomp in their processions. On equally slight grounds they identified Kṛishṇa, another god whom they saw worshipped, with Hêrakles; and whenever, as among the Sibae, they saw the skins of wild beasts, or clubs, or the like, they assumed that Hêrakles had at some time or other dwelt there."—Schwanb. p. 43.

which had to the eye the appearance of mountains, and were so contrived that they were planted with all sorts of trees, because his wife, who had been bred up in the land of Media, wished her surroundings to be like those of her early home.] Megasthenês also, *in the 4th book of his Indika*, makes mention of these things, and thereby endeavours to show that this king surpassed Hêrakles in courage and the greatness of his achievements, for he says that he conquered Libya and a great part of Ibêria.

Fragm. XLVIII. C.

Zonar. ed. Basil. 1557, T. I. p. 87.

Among the many old historians who mention Nabouchodonosor, Jôsephos enumerates Bêrôsos, Megasthenês, and Dioklês.

Fragm. XLVIII. D.

G. Syncell. T. I. p. 419, ed. Benn. (p. 221 ed. Paris, p. 177 ed. Venet.).

Megasthenês, in *his fourth book of the Indika*, represents Nabouchodonosor as mightier than Hêrakles, because with great courage and enterprise he conquered the greater part of Libya and Ibêria.

Fragm. XLIX.

Abyden. ap. *Euseb. Præp. Ev.* I. 41 (ed. Colon. 1688, p. 456 D).

Of Nabouchodrosor.

Megasthenês says that Nabouchodrosor, who was mightier than Hêrakles, undertook an expedition against Libya and Ibêria, and that having conquered them he planted a colony of these people in the parts lying to the right of Pontos.

FRAGM. L.

Arr. *Ind.* 7-9.

(See the translation of Arrian's *Indika.*)

FRAGM. L. B.

Plin. *Hist. Nat.* IX. 55.

Of Pearls.

Some writers allege that in swarms of oysters, as among bees, individuals distinguished for size and beauty act as leaders. These are of wonderful cunning in preventing themselves being caught, and are eagerly sought for by the divers. Should they be caught, the others are easily enclosed in the nets as they go wandering about. They are then put into earthen pots, where they are buried deep in salt. By this process the flesh is all eaten away, and the hard concretions, which are the pearls, drop down to the bottom.

FRAGM. LI.

Phlegon. *Mirab.* 33.

Of the Pandaian Land.

(Cf. Fragm. XXX. 6.)

Megasthenês says that the women of the Pandaian realm bear children when they are six years of age.

Fragm. L. C.

Plin. *Hist. Nat.* VI. xxi. 4-5.

Of the Ancient History of the Indians.

For the Indians stand almost alone among the nations in never having migrated from their own country. From the days of Father Bacchus to Alexander the Great their kings are reckoned at 154, whose reigns extend over 6451 years and 3 months.

Solin. 52. 5.

Father Bacchus was the first who invaded India, and was the first of all who triumphed over the vanquished Indians. From him to Alexander the Great 6451 years are reckoned with 3 months additional, the calculation being made by counting the kings who reigned in the intermediate period, to the number of 153.

Fragm. XLV.

Arr. VII. ii. 3-9.§

Of Kalanos and Mandanis.

This shows that Alexander, notwithstanding the terrible ascendancy which the passion for glory had acquired over him, was not altogether without a perception of the things that are better; for when he arrived at Taxila and saw the Indian

§ This fragment is an extract from Arrian's *Expedition of Alexander*, and not his *Indika* as stated (by an oversight) at p. 107. The translation is accordingly now inserted.

gymnosophists, a desire seized him to have one of these men brought into his presence, because he admired their endurance. The eldest of these sophists, with whom the others lived as disciples with a master, Dandamis by name, not only refused to go himself, but prevented the others going. He is said to have returned this for answer, that he also was the son of Zeus as much as Alexander himself was, and that he wanted nothing that was Alexander's (for he was well off in his present circumstances), whereas he saw those who were with him wandering over so much sea and land for no good got by it, and without any end coming to their many wanderings. He coveted, therefore, nothing Alexander had it in his power to give, nor, on the other hand, feared aught he could do to coerce him: for if he lived, India would suffice for him, yielding him her fruits in due season, and if he died, he would be delivered from his ill-assorted companion the body. Alexander accordingly did not put forth his hand to violence, knowing the man to be of an independent spirit. He is said, however, to have won over Kalanos, one of the sophists of that place, whom Megasthenês represents as a man utterly wanting in self-control, while the sophists themselves spoke opprobriously of Kalanos, because that, having left the happiness enjoyed among them, he went to serve another master than God.

DOUBTFUL FRAGMENTS.

Fragm. LII.

Ælian, *Hist. Anim.* XII. 8.

Of Elephants.

(Conf. Fragm. xxxvi. 10, xxxvii. 10.)

The elephant when feeding at large ordinarily drinks water, but when undergoing the fatigues of war is allowed wine,—not that sort, however, which comes from the grape, but another which is prepared from rice.|| The attendants even go in advance of their elephants and gather them flowers; for they are very fond of sweet perfumes, and they are accordingly taken out to the meadows, there to be trained under the influence of the sweetest fragrance. The animal selects the flowers according to their smell, and throws them as they are gathered into a basket which is held out by the trainer. This being filled, and harvest-work, so to speak, completed, he then bathes, and enjoys his bath with all the zest of a consummate voluptuary. On returning from bathing he is impatient to have his flowers, and if there is delay in bringing them he begins roaring, and will not taste a morsel of food till all the flowers he gathered are placed before him. This done, he takes the flowers out of the basket with his trunk and scatters them over the edge of his

|| Called *arak*, (which, however, is also applied to *tâḍi*); rum is now-a-days the beverage given it.

manger, and makes by this device their fine scent be, as it were, a relish to his food. He strews also a good quantity of them as litter over his stall, for he loves to have his sleep made sweet and pleasant.

The Indian elephants were nine cubits in height and five in breadth. The largest elephants in all the land were those called the Praisian, and next to these the Taxilan.¶

Fragm. LIII.

Ælian, *Hist. Anim.* III. 46.

Of a White Elephant.

(Cf. Fragm. xxxvi. 11, xxxvii. 11.)

An Indian elephant-trainer fell in with a white elephant-calf, which he brought when still quite young to his home, where he reared it, and gradually made it quite tame and rode upon it. He became much attached to the creature, which loved him in return, and by its affection requited him for its maintenance. Now the king of the Indians, having heard of this elephant, wanted to take it; but the owner, jealous of the love it had for him, and grieving much, no doubt, to think that another should become its master, refused to give it away, and made off at once to the

¶ This fragment is ascribed to Megasthenês both on account of the matter of it, and because it was undoubtedly from Megasthenês that Ælian borrowed the narrative preceding it (Fragm. xxxviii.) and that following it (Fragm. xxxv.).—Schwanbeck.

desert mounted on his favourite. The king was enraged at this, and sent men in pursuit, with orders to seize the elephant, and at the same time to bring back the Indian for punishment. Overtaking the fugitive they attempted to execute their purpose, but he resisted and attacked his assailants from the back of the elephant, which in the affray fought on the side of its injured master. Such was the state of matters at the first, but afterwards, when the Indian on being wounded slipped down to the ground, the elephant, true to his salt, bestrides him as soldiers in battle bestride a fallen comrade, whom they cover with their shields, kills many of the assailants, and puts the rest to flight. Then twining his trunk around his rearer he lifted him on to his back, and carried him home to the stall, and remained with him like a faithful friend with his friend, and showed him every kind attention.* [O men! how base are ye! ever dancing merrily when ye hear the music of the frying-pan, ever revelling in the banquet, but traitors in the hour of danger, and vainly and for nought sullying the sacred name of friendship.]

---

* Compare the account given in Plutarch's *Life of Alexander*, of the elephant of Pôros:—"This elephant during the whole battle gave extraordinary proofs of his sagacity and care of the king's person. As long as that prince was able to fight, he defended him with great courage, and repulsed all assailants; and when he perceived him ready to sink under the multitude of darts, and the wounds with which he was covered, to prevent his falling off he kneeled down in the softest manner, and with his proboscis gently drew every dart out of his body."

FRAGM. LIV.

Pseudo-Origen, *Philosoph.* 24, ed. Delarue, Paris, 1733, vol. I. p. 904.

Of the Bráhmaṇs and their Philosophy.

(Cf. Fragm. xli., xliv., xlv.)

Of the Brachhmans in India.

There is among the Brachhmaṇs in India a sect of philosophers who adopt an independent life, and abstain from animal food and all victuals cooked by fire, being content to subsist upon fruits, which they do not so much as gather from the trees, but pick up when they have dropped to the ground, and their drink is the water of the river Tagabena.† Throughout life they go about naked, saying that the body has been given by the Deity as a covering for the soul.‡ They hold that God is light,§ but not such light as we see

---

† Probably the Sanskrit Tungaveṇâ, now the Tungabhadra, a large affluent of the Kṛishṇâ.

‡ *Vide Ind. Ant.* vol. V. p. 128, note †. A doctrine of the Vedânta school of philosophy, according to which the soul is incased as in a sheath, or rather a succession of sheaths. The first or inner case is the intellectual one, composed of the sheer and simple elements uncombined, and consisting of the intellect joined with the five senses. The second is the mental sheath, in which mind is joined with the preceding, or, as some hold, with the organs of action. The third comprises these organs and the vital faculties, and is called the organic or vital case. These three sheaths (*kośa*) constitute the subtle frame which attends the soul in its transmigrations. The exterior case is composed of the coarse elements combined in certain proportions, and is called the gross body. See Colebrooke's *Essay on the Philosophy of the Hindus*, Cowell's ed. pp. 395-6.

§ The affinity between God and light is the burden of the *Gâyatri* or holiest verse of the Veda.

with the eye, nor such as the sun or fire, but God is with them the Word,—by which term they do not mean articulate speech, but the discourse of reason, whereby the hidden mysteries of knowledge are discerned by the wise. This light, however, which they call the Word, and think to be God, is, they say, known only by the Brachhmans themselves, because they alone have discarded vanity,|| which is the outermost covering of the soul. The members of this sect regard death with contemptuous indifference, and, as we have seen already, they always pronounce the name of the Deity with a tone of peculiar reverence, and adore him with hymns. They neither have wives nor beget children. Persons who desire to lead a life like theirs cross over from the other side of the river, and remain with them for good, never returning to their own country. These also are called Brachhmans, although they do not follow the same mode of life, for there are women in the country, from whom the native inhabitants are sprung, and of these women they beget offspring. With regard to the Word, which they call God, they hold that it is corporeal, and that it wears the body as its external covering, just as

|| κενοδοξία, which probably translates *ahankâra*, literally 'egotism,' and hence 'self-consciousness,' the peculiar and appropriate function of which is selfish conviction; that is, a belief that in perception and meditation 'I' am concerned; that the objects of sense concern Me—in short, that I AM. The knowledge, however, which comes from comprehending that Being which has self-existence completely destroys the ignorance which says 'I am.'

one wears the woollen surcoat, and that when it divests itself of the body with which it is enwrapped it becomes manifest to the eye. There is war, the Brachhmans hold, in the body wherewith they are clothed, and they regard the body as being the fruitful source of wars, and, as we have already shown, fight against it like soldiers in battle contending against the enemy. They maintain, moreover, that all men are held in bondage, like prisoners of war,¶ to their own innate enemies, the sensual appetites, gluttony, anger, joy, grief, longing desire, and such like, while it is only the man who has triumphed over these enemies who goes to God. Dandamis accordingly, to whom Alexander the Makedonian paid a visit, is spoken of by the Brachhmans as a god because he conquered in the warfare against the body, and on the other hand they condemn Kalanos as one who had impiously apostatized from their philosophy. The Brachhmans, therefore, when they have shuffled off the body, see the pure sunlight as fish see it when they spring up out of the water into the air.

¶ Compare Plato, *Phœdo*, cap. 32, where Sokratês speaks of the soul as at present confined in the body as in a species of prison. This was a doctrine of the Pythagoreans, whose philosophy, even in its most striking peculiarities, bears such a close resemblance to the Indian as greatly to favour the supposition that it was directly borrowed from it. There was even a tradition that Pythagoras had visited India.

FRAGM. LV.

Pallad. *de Bragmanibus*, pp. 8, 20 *et seq*. ed. Londin. 1668.
(*Camerar. libell. gnomolog.* pp. 116, 124 *et seq.*)

Of Kalanos and Mandanis.

(Cf. Fragm. xli. 19, xliv., xlv.)

They (the Bragmanes) subsist upon such fruits as they can find, and on wild herbs, which the earth spontaneously produces, and drink only water. They wander about in the woods, and sleep at night on pallets of the leaves of trees. . . .

. . . .

"Kalanos, then, your false friend, held this opinion, but he is despised and trodden upon by us. By you, however, accomplice as he was in causing many evils to you all, he is honoured and worshipped, while from our society he has been contemptuously cast out as unprofitable. And why not? when everything which we trample under foot is an object of admiration to the lucre-loving Kalanos, your worthless friend, but no friend of ours,—a miserable creature, and more to be pitied than the unhappiest wretch, for by setting his heart on lucre he wrought the perdition of his soul! Hence he seemed neither worthy of us, nor worthy of the friendship of God, and hence he neither was content to revel away life in the woods beyond all reach of care, nor was he cheered with the hope of a blessed hereafter: for by his love of money he slew the very life of his miserable soul.

"We have, however, amongst us a sage called Dandamis, whose home is the woods, where he lies on a pallet of leaves, and where he has nigh at hand the fountain of peace, whereof he drinks, sucking, as it were, the pure breast of a mother."

King Alexander, accordingly, when he heard of all this, was desirous of learning the doctrines of the sect, and so he sent for this Dandamis, as being their teacher and president . . . .

Onesikratês was therefore despatched to fetch him, and when he found the great sage he said, "Hail to thee, thou teacher of the Bragmanes. The son of the mighty god Zeus, king Alexander, who is the sovereign lord of all men, asks you to go to him, and if you comply, he will reward you with great and splendid gifts, but if you refuse will cut off your head."

Dandamis, with a complacent smile, heard him to the end, but did not so much as lift up his head from his couch of leaves, and while still retaining his recumbent attitude returned this scornful answer:—"God, the supreme king, is never the author of insolent wrong, but is the creator of light, of peace, of life, of water, of the body of man, and of souls, and these he receives when death sets them free, being in no way subject to evil desire. He alone is the god of my homage, who abhors slaughter and instigates no wars. But Alexander is not God, since he must taste of death; and how can such as he be the world's master, who has not yet reached the further shore of the river Tiberoboas, and has not yet seated himself on a throne of universal dominion? Moreover, Alexander has neither as yet entered living into Hades,* nor does he know the course of the sun through the central regions of the earth, while the nations on its boundaries have not so much as heard his name.† If his present dominions are not capacious enough for his desire, let him cross the Ganges river, and he will find a region able to sustain men if the country on our side be too narrow to hold him. Know this, however, that what Alexander offers me, and the gifts he promises, are all things to me utterly useless; but the things which I prize, and find of real use and worth, are these leaves which are my house, these blooming plants which supply me with dainty food, and the water which is my drink, while all other possessions and things, which are amassed with anxious care, are wont to prove ruinous to those who amass them, and cause only sorrow and vexation, with which every poor mortal is fully fraught. But as for me, I lie upon the forest leaves, and, having nothing which requires guarding, close my eyes in tranquil slumber; whereas had I gold to guard, that would banish sleep. The earth supplies me with everything, even as a mother her child with milk. I go wherever I please, and there are no

* ζῶν ἐν ᾅδου οὐδέπω παρῆλθεν. The Latin version has *non zonam Gadem transiit*, 'has not crossed *the zone of Cadiz*.'

† The text here is so corrupt as to be almost untranslatable. I have therefore rendered from the Latin, though not quite closely.

cares with which I am forced to cumber myself, against my will. Should Alexander cut off my head, he cannot also destroy my soul. My head alone, now silent, will remain, but the soul will go away to its Master, leaving the body like a torn garment upon the earth, whence also it was taken. I then, becoming spirit, shall ascend to my God, who enclosed us in flesh, and left us upon the earth to prove whether when here below we shall live obedient to his ordinances, and who also will require of us, when we depart hence to his presence, an account of our life, since he is judge of all proud wrong-doing; for the groans of the oppressed become the punishments of the oppressors.

"Let Alexander, then, terrify with these threats those who wish for gold and for wealth, and who dread death, for against us these weapons are both alike powerless, since the Bragmanes neither love gold nor fear death. Go, then, and tell Alexander this: 'Dandamis has no need of aught that is yours, and therefore will not go to you, but if you want anything from Dandamis come you to him.' "‡

Alexander, on receiving from Onesikratês a report of the interview, felt a stronger desire than ever to see Dandamis, who, though old and naked, was the only antagonist in whom he, the conqueror of many nations, had found more than his match, &c.

‡ "Others say Dandamis entered into no discourse with the messengers, but only asked 'why Alexander had taken so long a journey?' "—Plutarch's *Alexander*.

FRAGM. LV. B.

Ambrosius, *De Moribus Brachmanorum*, pp. 62, 68 *et seq.* ed. Pallad. Londin. 1668.

Of Calanus and Mandanis.

They (*the Brachmans*) eat what they find on the ground, such as leaves of trees and wild herbs, like cattle. . . . .

"Calanus is your friend, but he is despised and trodden upon by us. He, then, who was the author of many evils among you, is honoured and worshipped by you; but since he is of no importance he is rejected by us, and those things we certainly do not seek, please Calanus because of his greediness for money. But he was not ours, a man such as has miserably injured and lost his soul, on which account he is plainly unworthy to be a friend either of God or of ours, nor has he deserved security among the woods in this world, nor can he hope for the glory which is promised in the future."

When the emperor Alexander came to the forests, he was not able to see Dandamis as he passed through. . . .

When, therefore, the above-mentioned messenger came to Dandamis, he addressed him thus :—"The emperor Alexander, the son of the great Jupiter, who is lord of the human race, has ordered that you should hasten to him, for if you come, he will give you many gifts, but if you refuse he will behead you as a punishment for your contempt." When these words came to the ears of Dandamis, he rose not from his leaves whereon he lay, but reclining and smiling he replied in this way :—"The greatest God," he said, "can do injury to no one, but restores again the light of life to those who have departed. Accordingly he alone is my lord who forbids murder and excites no wars. But Alexander is no God, for he himself will have to die. How, then, can he be the lord of all, who has not yet crossed the river Tyberoboas, nor has made the whole world his abode, nor crossed the zone of Gades, nor has beheld the course of the sun in the centre of the world? Therefore many nations do not yet even know his name. If, however, the country he possesses cannot contain him, let him cross our river and he will find a soil which is able to support men. All those things Alexander promises would be useless to me if he gave them: I have leaves for a house, live on the herbs at hand and water to drink; other things collected with labour, and which perish and yield nothing but sorrow to those seeking them or possessing them,—these I despise. I therefore now rest secure, and with closed eyes I care for nothing. If I wish to keep gold, I destroy my sleep; Earth supplies me with everything, as a mother does to her child. Wherever I wish to go, I proceed, and wherever I do not wish to be, no necessity of care can force me to go. And if he wish to cut off my head, he cannot take my soul; he will only take the fallen head, but the departing soul will leave the head like a portion of some garment, and will restore it to whence it received it, namely, to the earth. But when I shall have become a spirit I shall ascend to God, who has enclosed it within this flesh. When he did this he wished to try us, how, after leaving him, we would live in this world. And afterwards, when we shall have returned to him, he will demand from us an account of this life. Standing by him I shall see my injury, and shall contemplate his judgment on those who injured me: for the sighs and groans of the injured become the punishments of the oppressors.

"Let Alexander threaten with this them that desire riches or fear death, both of which I despise. For Brachmans neither love gold nor dread death. Go, therefore, and tell Alexander this:—'Dandamis seeks nothing of yours, but if you think you need something of his, disdain not to go to him.'"

When Alexander heard these words through the interpreter, he wished the more to see such a man, since he, who had subdued many nations, was overcome by an old naked man, &c.

Fragm. LVI.

Plin. *Hist. Nat.* VI. 21. 8—23. 11.

List of the Indian Races.§

The other journeys made thence (*from the Hyphasis*) for Seleukos Nikator are as follows:— 168 miles to the Hesidrus, and to the river Jomanes as many (some copies add 5 miles); from thence to the Ganges 112 miles. 119 miles to Rhodopha (others give 325 miles for this distance). To the town Kalinipaxa 167—500. Others give 265 miles. Thence to the confluence of the Jomanes and Ganges 625 miles (many add 13

§ This list Pliny has borrowed for the most part from Megasthenês. Cf. Schwanbeck, pp. 16 *seq.*, 57 *seq.*

miles), and to the town Palimbothra 425. To the mouth of the Ganges 738 miles.||

|| According to the MSS. 638 or 637 miles. The places mentioned in this famous itinerary all lay on the Royal Road, which ran from the Indus to Palibothra. They have been thus identified. The Hesidrus is now the Satlej, and the point of departure lay immediately below its junction with the Hyphasis (now the Biâs). The direct route thence (*viâ* Ludhiânâ, Sirhind, and Ambâlâ) conducted the traveller to the ferry of the Jomanes, now the Jamnâ, in the neighbourhood of the present Bureah, whence the road led to the Ganges at a point which, to judge from the distance given (112 miles), must have been near the site of the far-famed Hastinapura. The next stage to be reached was Rhodopha, the position of which, both its name and its distance from the Ganges (119 miles) combine to fix at Dabhai, a small town about 12 miles to the south of Anupshahr. Kalinipaxa, the next stage, Mannert and Lassen would identify with Kanauj (the Kanyâkubja of Sanskṛit); but M. de St.-Martin, objecting to this that Pliny was not likely to have designated so important and so celebrated a city by so obscure an appellation, finds a site for it in the neighbourhood on the banks of the Ikshumati, a river of Panchâla mentioned in the great Indian poems. This river, he remarks, must also have been called the Kalinadî, as the names of it still in current use, Kalinî and Kalindri, prove. Now, as 'paxa' transliterates the Sanskṛit 'paksha,' *a side*, Kalinipaxa, to judge from its name, must designate a town lying near the Kalinadî.

The figures which represent the distances have given rise to much dispute, some of them being inconsistent either with others, or with the real distances. The text, accordingly, has generally been supposed to be corrupt, so far at least as the figures are concerned. M. de St.-Martin, however, accepting the figures nearly as they stand, shows them to be fairly correct. The first difficulty presents itself in the words, "*Others give* 325 *miles for this distance.*" By '*this distance*' cannot be meant the distance between the Ganges and Rhodopha, but between the Hesidrus and Rhodopha, which the addition of the figures shows to be 399 miles. The shorter estimate of others (325 miles) measures the length of a more direct route by way of Paṭiâlâ, Thanêśvara, Panipat, and Dehli. The next difficulty has probably been occasioned by a corruption of the text. It lies in the words "Ad Calinipaxa oppidum CLXVII. D. Alii CCLXV. mill." The numeral D has generally been taken to mean 500 paces, or half a Roman mile, making the translation run thus :—"To Kalinipaxa

The races which we may enumerate without being tedious, from the chain of Emodus, of which

---

167½ miles. Others give 265 miles." But M. de St.-Martin prefers to think that the D has, by some mangling of the text, been detached from the beginning of the second number, with which it formed the number DLXV., and been appended to the first, being led to this conclusion on finding that the number 565 sums up almost to a nicety the distance from the Hesidrus to Kalinipaxa, as thus:—

From the Hesidrus to the Jomanes......	168 miles.
From the Jomanes to the Ganges.........	112 „
From the Ganges to Rhodopha	119 „
From Rhodopha to Kalinipaxa	167 „
Total...	566 miles.

Pliny's carelessness in confounding total with partial distances has created the next difficulty, which lies in his stating that the distance from Kalinipaxa to the confluence of the Jomanes and the Ganges is 625 miles, while in reality it is only about 227. The figures may be corrupt, but it is much more probable that they represent the distance of some stage on the route remoter from the confluence of the rivers than Kalinipaxa. This must have been the passage of the Jomanes, for the distance—

From the Jomanes to the Ganges is ...	112 miles.
Thence to Rhodopha	119 „
Thence to Kalinipaxa	167 „
Thence to the confluence of the rivers.	227 „
Total...	625 miles.

This is exactly equal to 5000 stadia, the length of the Indian Mesopotamia or Doâb, the Panchâla of Sanskṛit geography, and the Antarvêda of lexicographers.

The foregoing conclusions M. de St.-Martin has summed up in the table annexed:—

	Roman miles.		Stadia.
From the Hesidrus to the Jomanes.	168		1344
From the Jomanes to the Ganges...	112		896
Thence to Rhodopha	119		952
From the Hesidrus to Rhodopha by a more direct route		325	2600
From Rhodopha to Kalinipaxa......	167		1336
Total distance from the Hesidrus to Kalinipaxa		565	4520
From Kalinipaxa to the confluence of the Jomanes and Ganges	(227)		(1816)
Total distance from the passage of the Jomanes to its confluence with the Ganges		625	5000

a spur is called Imaus (meaning in the native language *snowy*),¶ are the Isari, Cosyri, Izgi, and on the hills the Chisiotosagi,* and

---

Pliny assigns 425 miles as the distance from the confluence of the rivers to Palibothra, but, as it is in reality only 248, the figures have probably been altered. He gives, lastly, 638 miles as the distance from Palibothra to the mouth of the Ganges, which agrees closely with the estimate of Megasthenês, who makes it 5000 stadia—if that indeed was his estimate, and not 6000 stadia as Strabo in one passage alleges it was. The distance by land from Pâṭnâ to Tamluk (Tamralipta, the old port of the Ganges' mouth) is 445 English or 480 Roman miles. The distance by the river, which is sinuous, is of course much greater. See *E'tude sur le Géographie Grecque et Latine de l'Inde*, par P. V. de Saint-Martin, pp. 271-278.

¶ By Emodus was generally designated that part of the Himâlayan range which extended along Nepâl and Bhûtan and onward toward the ocean. Other forms of the name are Emoda, Emodon, Hemodes. Lassen derives the word from the Sanskṛit *haimavata*, in Prâkṛit *haimôta*, 'snowy.' If this be so, Hemodus is the more correct form. Another derivation refers the word to 'Hêmâdri' (*hema*, 'gold,' and *adri*, 'mountain'), the 'golden mountains,'—so called either because they were thought to contain gold mines, or because of the aspect they presented when their snowy peaks reflected the golden effulgence of sunset. Imaus represents the Sanskṛit *himavata*, 'snowy.' The name was applied at first by the Greeks to the Hindû Kush and the Himâlayas, but was in course of time transferred to the Bolor range. This chain, which runs north and south, was regarded by the ancients as dividing Northern Asia into 'Skythia intra Imaum' and 'Skythia extra Imaum,' and it has formed for ages the boundary between China and Turkestân.

* These four tribes were located somewhere in Kaśmîr or its immediate neighbourhood. The Isari are unknown, but are probably the same as the Brysari previously mentioned by Pliny. The Cosyri are easily to be identified with the Khasîra mentioned in the *Mahâbhârata* as neighbours of the Daradas and Kaśmîras. Their name, it has been conjectured, survives in *Khâchar*, one of the three great divisions of the Kâṭhîs of Gujarât, who appear to have come originally from the Panjâb. The Izgi are mentioned in Ptolemy, under the name of the Sizyges, as a people of Sêrikê. This is, however, a mistake, as they inhabited the alpine region which extends above Kaśmîr towards the

the Brachmanæ, a name comprising many tribes, among which are the Maccocalingæ.†

---

north and north-west. The Chisiotosagi or Chirotosagi are perhaps identical with the Chiconæ (whom Pliny elsewhere mentions), in spite of the addition to their name of 'sagi,' which may have merely indicated them to be a branch of the Śâkas,—that is, the Skythians,—by whom India was overrun before the time of its conquest by the Âryans. They are mentioned in Manu X. 44 together with the Pauṇḍrakas, Odras, Drâvidas, Kâmbojas, Yavanas, Paradas, Pahlavas, Chînas, Kîratas, Daradas, and Khaśas. If Chirotosagi be the right reading of their name, there can be little doubt of their identity with the Kîratas.—See P. V. de St.-Martin's work already quoted, pp. 195-197. But for the *Khâchars*, see *Ind. Ant.* vol. IV. p. 323.

† v. l. Bracmanæ. Pliny at once transports his readers from the mountains of Kaśmîr to the lower part of the valley of the Ganges. Here he places the Brachmanæ, whom he takes to be, not what they actually were, the leading caste of the population, but a powerful race composed of many tribes—the Maccocalingæ being of the number. This tribe, as well as the Gangaridæ-Kalingæ, and the Modogalingæ afterwards mentioned, are subdivisions of the Kalingæ, a widely diffused race, which spread at one time from the delta of the Ganges all along the eastern coast of the peninsula, though afterwards they did not extend southward beyond Orissa. In the *Mahâbhârata* they are mentioned as occupying, along with the Vangas (from whom Bengal is named) and three other leading tribes, the region which lies between Magadha and the sea. The Maccocalingæ, then, are the *Magha* of the Kalingæ. "Magha," says M. de St.-Martin, "is the name of one of the non-Âryan tribes of greatest importance and widest diffusion in the lower Gangetic region, where it is broken up into several special groups extending from Arakan and Western Asam, where it is found under the name of *Mogh* (Anglicè *Mugs*), as far as to the *Mâghars* of the central valleys of Nepâl, to the *Maghayas*, *Magahis*, or *Maghyas* of Southern Bahâr (the ancient Magadha), to the ancient *Magra* of Bengal, and to the *Magora* of Orissa. These last, by their position, may properly be taken to represent our Maccocalingæ." "The Modogalingæ," continues the same author, "find equally their representatives in the ancient *Mada*, a colony which the Book of Manu mentions in his enumeration of the impure tribes of Âryâvarta, and which he names by the side of the Ândhra, another people of the lower Ganges. The Monghyr inscription, which belongs to the earlier part of

The river **P r i n a s**‡ and the **C a i n a s** (which flows into the Ganges) are both navigable.§ The tribes called **C a l i n g æ** are nearest the sea, and higher up are the **M a n d e i**, and the **M a l l i** in whose

---

the 8th century of our era, also names the *Meda* as a low tribe of this region (*As. Res.* vol. I. p. 126, Calcutta, 1788), and, what is remarkable, their name is found joined to that of the Andhra (Andharaka), precisely as in the text of Manu. Pliny assigns for their habitation a large island of the Ganges; and the word Galinga (for Kalinga), to which their name is attached, necessarily places this island towards the sea-board—perhaps in the Delta."

The Gangaridæ or Gangarides occupied the region corresponding roughly with that now called Lower Bengal, and consisted of various indigenous tribes, which in the course of time became more or less Âryanized. As no word is found in Sanskrit to which their name corresponds, it has been supposed of Greek invention (Lassen, *Ind. Alt.* vol. II. p. 201), but erroneously, for it must have been current at the period of the Makedonian invasion: since Alexander, in reply to inquiries regarding the south country, was informed that the region of the Ganges was inhabited by two principal nations, the Prasii and the Gangarîdæ. M. de St.-Martin thinks that their name has been preserved almost identically in that of the Gonghrîs of South Bahâr, whose traditions refer their origin to Tirhût; and he would identify their royal city *Parthalis* (or *Portalis*) with Varddhana (contraction of Varddhamâna), now Bardwân. Others, however, place it, as has been elsewhere stated, on the Mahânadî. In Ptolemy their capital is Gangê, which must have been situated near where Calcutta now stands. The Gangarides are mentioned by Virgil, *Georg.* III. 27:—

In foribus pugnam ex auro solidoque elephanto
Gangaridum faciam, victorisque arma Quirini.

"High o'er the gate in elephant and gold
The crowd shall Cæsar's Indian war behold."

(Dryden's translation.)

‡ v. l. Pumas. The Prinas is probably the Tâmasâ or Tonsa, which in the Purâṇas is called the Parṇâśâ. The Cainas, notwithstanding the objections of Schwanbeck, must be identified with the Cane, which is a tributary of the Jamnâ.

§ For the identification of these and other affluents of the Ganges see *Notes on Arrian*, c. iv., *Ind. Ant.* vol. V. p. 331.

country is Mount Mallus, the boundary of all that district being the Ganges.

(22.) This river, according to some, rises from uncertain sources, like the Nile,‖ and inundates similarly the countries lying along its course; others say that it rises on the Skythian mountains, and has nineteen tributaries, of which, besides those already mentioned, the Condochates, Erannoboas,¶ Cosoagus, and Sonus are navigable. Others again assert that it issues forth at once with loud roar from its fountain, and after tumbling down a steep and rocky channel is received immediately on reaching the level plains into a lake, whence it flows out with a gentle current, being at the narrowest eight miles, and on the average a hundred stadia, in breadth, and never of less depth than twenty paces (one hundred feet) in the final part of its course, which is through the country of the Gangarides. The royal* city of the Calingæ is called Parthalis. Over their king 60,000 foot-soldiers,

‖ For an account of the different theories regarding the source of the Ganges see Smith's *Dict. of Class. Geog.*

¶ *Condochatem, Erannoboam.*—v. l. Canucham (Vamam), Erranoboan.

* *regia.*—v. l. regio. The common reading, however—"Gangaridum Calingarum. Regia," &c., makes the Gangarides a branch of the Kalingæ. This is probably the correct reading, for, as General Cunningham states (*Anc. Geog. of Ind.* pp. 518-519), certain inscriptions speak of 'Tri-Kalinga,' or 'the Three Kalingas.' "The name of Tri-Kalinga," he adds, "is probably old, as Pliny mentions the *Macco-Calingæ* and the *Gangarides-Calingæ* as separate peoples from the Calingæ, while the *Mahâbhârata* names the Kalingas three separate times, and each time in con-

1000† horsemen, 700 elephants keep watch and ward in "procinct of war."

For among the more civilized Indian communities life is spent in a great variety of separate occupations. Some till the soil, some are soldiers, some traders; the noblest and richest take part in the direction of state affairs, administer justice, and sit in council with the kings. A fifth class devotes itself to the philosophy prevalent in the country, which almost assumes the form of a religion, and the members always put an end to their life by a voluntary death on a burning funeral pile.‡ In addition to these classes there is one half-wild, which is constantly engaged in a task of immense labour, beyond the power of words to describe—that of hunting and

---

junction with different peoples." (H. H. Wilson in *Vishnu Purâṇa*, 1st ed. pp. 185, 187 note, and 188.) As Tri-Kalinga thus corresponds with the great province of Telingâna, it seems probable that the name of Telingâna may be only a slightly contracted form of Tri-Kalingâna, or 'the Three Kalingas.'

† *LX. mill.*—v. l. LXX. mill.

‡ Lucian, in his satirical piece on the death of Peregrînos (cap. 25), refers to this practice:—"But what is the motive which prompts this man (Peregrînos) to fling himself into the flames? God knows it is simply that he may show off how he can endure pain as do the Brachmans, to whom it pleased Theagenês to liken him, just as if India had not her own crop of fools and vain-glorious persons. But let him by all means imitate the Brachmans, for, as Onesikritos informs us, who was the pilot of Alexander's fleet and saw Kalanos burned, they do not immolate themselves by leaping into the flames, but when the pyre is made they stand close beside it perfectly motionless, and suffer themselves to be gently broiled; then decorously ascending the pile they are burned to death, and never swerve, even ever so little, from their recumbent position."

taming elephants. They employ these animals in ploughing and for riding on, and regard them as forming the main part of their stock in cattle. They employ them in war and in fighting for their country. In choosing them for war, regard is had to their age, strength, and size.

There is a very large island in the Ganges which is inhabited by a single tribe called Modogalingæ.§ Beyond are situated the Modubæ, Molindæ, the Uberæ with a handsome town of the same name, the Galmodroësi, Preti, Calissæ,|| Sasuri, Passalæ, Colubæ, Orxulæ, Abali, Taluctæ.¶ The king of

---

§ vv. ll. modo Galingam, Modogalicam.

|| *Calissæ.*—v. l. Aclissæ.

¶ These tribes were chiefly located in the regions between the left bank of the Ganges and the Himâlayas. Of the Galmodroësi, Preti, Calissæ, Sasuri, and Orxulæ nothing is known, nor can their names be identified with any to be found in Sanskṛit literature. The Modubæ represent beyond doubt the Moutiba, a people mentioned in the *Aitarêya Brâhmaṇa* along with other non-Âryan tribes which occupied the country north of the Ganges at the time when the Brâhmaṇs established their first settlements in the country. The Molindæ are mentioned as the Malada in the Purâṇic lists, but no further trace of them is met with. The Uberæ must be referred to the Bhars, a numerous race spread over the central districts of the region spoken of, and extending as far as to Assam. The name is pronounced differently in different districts, and variously written, as Bors or Bhors, Bhowris, Barriias and Bhârhîyas, Bareyas, Baoris, Bharais, &c. The race, though formerly powerful, is now one of the lowest classes of the population. The Passalæ are identified as the inhabitants of Panchâla, which, as already stated, was the old name of the Doâb. The Colubæ respond to the Kâulûta or Kolûta—mentioned in the 4th book of the *Râmâyaṇa*, in the enumeration of the races of the west, also in the *Varâha Sañhitâ* in the list of the people of the north-west, and in the Indian drama called the *Mudra Râkshasa*, of which the hero is the well-known Chandragupta. They were set-

these keeps under arms 50,000 foot-soldiers, 4000* cavalry, and 400 elephants. Next come the Andaræ,† a still more powerful race, which possesses numerous villages, and thirty towns defended by walls and towers, and which supplies its king with an army of 100,000 infantry, 2000 cavalry, and 1000 elephants. Gold is very abundant among the Dardæ, and silver among the Setæ.‡

---

tled not far from the Upper Jamnâ. About the middle of the 7th century they were visited by the famous Chinese traveller Hiwen-Thsâng, who writes their name as Kiu-lu-to. Yule, however, places the Passalæ in the south-west of Tirhut, and the Kolubæ on the Kondochates (Gandakî) in the north-east of Gorakhpur and north-west of Sâran. The Abali answer perhaps to the Gvallas or Halvaïs of South Bahâr and of the hills which covered the southern parts of the ancient Magadha. The Taluctæ are the people of the kingdom of Tâmralipta mentioned in the *Mahâbhârata*. In the writings of the Buddhists of Ceylon the name appears as Tamalitti, corresponding to the Tamluk of the present day. Between these two forms of the name that given by Pliny is evidently the connecting link. Tamluk lies to the south-west of Calcutta, from which it is distant in a direct line about 35 miles. It was in old times the main emporium of the trade carried on between Gangetic India and Ceylon.

* *IV. M.*—v. l. III. M.

† The Andaræ are readily identified with the Andhra of Sanskṛit—a great and powerful nation settled originally in the Dekhaṇ between the middle part of the courses of the Godâvarî and the Kṛishṇâ rivers, but which, before the time of Megasthenês, had spread their sway towards the north as far as the upper course of the Narmadâ (Nerbudda), and, as has been already indicated, the lower districts of the Gangetic basin. *Vide Ind. Ant.* vol. V. p. 176. For a notice of Andhra (the modern Telingâna) see General Cunningham's *Anc. Geog. of Ind.* pp. 527-530.

‡ Pliny here reverts to where he started from in his enumeration of the tribes. The Setæ are the Sâta or Sâtaka of Sanskṛit geography, which locates them in the neighbourhood of the Daradas. [According to Yule, however, they are the Sanskṛit Sekas, and he places them on the Banâs about Jhajpur, south-east from Ajmir.—Ed. *Ind. Ant.*]

But the P r a s i i surpass in power and glory every other people, not only in this quarter, but one may say in all India, their capital being P a l i b o t h r a, a very large and wealthy city, after which some call the people itself the P a l i b o t h r i,—nay, even the whole tract along the Ganges. Their king has in his pay a standing army of 600,000 foot-soldiers, 30,000 cavalry, and 9000 elephants : whence may be formed some conjecture as to the vastness of his resources.

After these, but more inland, are the M o n e d e s and S u a r i,§ in whose country is Mount M a l e u s, on which shadows fall towards the north in winter, and towards the south in summer, for six months alternately.‖ Baeton asserts that the north pole in these parts is seen but once in the year, and only for fifteen days ; while Megasthenês says that the same thing happens in many parts of India. The south pole is called by the Indians D r a m a s a. The river J o m a n e s flows through the P a l i b o t h r i into the Ganges between the towns M e t h o r a and C a r i s o b o r a.¶ In the

§ The Monedes or Mandei are placed by Yule about Gangpur, on the upper waters of the Brâhmaṇî, S.W. of Chhutia Nâgpur. Lassen places them S. of the Mahânadi about Sonpur, where Yule has the Suari or Sabaræ, the Śavara of Sanskṛit authors, which Lassen places between Sonpur and Singhbhûm. See *Ind. Ant.* vol. VI. note §, p. 127.—Ed. *Ind. Ant.*

‖ This, of course, can only occur at the equator, from which the southern extremity of India is about 500 miles distant.

¶ Palibothri must denote here the subjects of the realm of which Palibothra was the capital, and not merely the inhabitants of that city, as Rennel and others supposed,

parts which lie southward from the Ganges the inhabitants, already swarthy, are deeply coloured by the sun, though not scorched black like the Ethiopians. The nearer they approach the Indus the more plainly does their complexion betray the influence of the sun.

The Indus skirts the frontiers of the Prasii, whose mountain tracts are said to be inhabited by the Pygmies.* Artemidorus† sets down the distance between the two rivers at 121 miles.

(23.) The Indus, called by the inhabitants Sindus, rising on that spur of Mount Caucasus which is called Paropamisus, from sources

---

and so fixed its site at the confluence of the Ganges and Jamunâ. Methora is easily identified with Mathurâ. Carisobora is read otherwise as Chrysobon, Cyrisoborca, Cleisoboras. "This city," says General Cunningham, "has not yet been identified, but I feel satisfied that it must be *Vrindâvana*, 16 miles to the north of Mathurâ. *Vrindâvana* means 'the grove of the basil-trees,' which is famed all over India as the scene of Kṛishṇa's sports with the milkmaids. But the earlier name of the place was *Kâlikavârtta*, or 'Kalika's whirlpool.' . . . Now the Latin name of Clisobora is also written *Carisobora* and *Cyrisoborka* in different MSS., from which I infer that the original spelling was *Kalisoborka*, or, by a slight change of two letters, *Kalikoborta* or *Kâlikâbarta*." *Anc. Geog. of Ind.* p. 375. [*Carisobora*—vv. ll. Chrysoban, Cyrisoborca. This is the Kleisobora of Arrian (*ante*, vol. V. p. 89), which Yule places at Batesar, and Lassen at Agra, which he makes the Sanskṛit Kṛishṇapura. Wilkins (*As. Res.* vol. V. p. 270) says Clisobora is now called "Mugu-Nagar by the Musulmans, and Kalisapura by the Hindus." *Vide Ind. Ant.* vol. VI. p. 249, note ‡.—Ed. *Ind. Ant.*]

* *Vide Ind. Ant.* vol. VI. p. 133, note †.—Ed. *Ind. Ant.*

† A Greek geographer of Ephesus, whose date is about 100 B.C. His valuable work on geography, called a *Periplûs*, was much quoted by the ancient writers, but with the exception of some fragments is now lost.

fronting the sunrise,‡ receives also itself nineteen rivers, of which the most famous are the H y d a s p e s, which has four tributaries; the C a n t a b r a,§ which has three; the A c e s i n e s and the H y p a s i s, which are both navigable; but nevertheless, having no very great supply of water, it is nowhere broader than fifty stadia, or deeper than fifteen paces.|| It forms an extremely large island, which is called P r a s i a n e, and a smaller one, called P a t a l e.¶ Its stream, which is navigable, by the lowest estimates, for 1240 miles, turns westward as if following more or less closely the course of the sun, and then falls into the ocean. The measure of the coast line from the mouth of the Ganges to this river I shall set down as it is generally given, though none of the computations agree with each other. From the mouth of the Ganges to Cape C a l i n g o n and the town of D a n d a g u l a* 625 miles;†

---

‡ The real sources of the Indus were unknown to the Greeks. The principal stream rises to the north of the Kailâsa mountain (which figures in Hindu mythology as the mansion of the gods and Śiva's paradise) in lat. 32°, long. 81° 30', at an elevation of about 20,000 feet.

§ The Chandrabhâga or Akesinês, now the Chenâb.

|| For remarks on the tributaries of the Indus see *Notes on Arrian*, chap. iv.,—*Ind. Ant.* vol. V. pp. 331-333.

¶ See *Ind. Ant.* vol. V. p. 330. Yule identifies the former of these with the area enclosed by the Nara from above Rohri to Haidarâbâd, and the delta of the Indus.—Ed. *Ind. Ant.*

* v. l. Dandaguda. Cape Kalingon is identified by Yule as Point Godâvarî.—Ed. *Ind. Ant.*

† "Both the distance and the name point to the great port town of *Coringa*, as the promontory of *Coringon*, which is situated on a projecting point of land at the

to Tropina 1225;‡ to the cape of Perimula,§ where there is the greatest emporium of trade in India, 750 miles; to the town in the island of Patala mentioned above, 620 miles.

The hill-tribes between the Indus and the Iomanes are the Cesi; the Cetriboni, who live in the woods; then the Megallæ, whose king is master of five hundred elephants and an army of horse and foot of unknown strength; the Chrysei, the Parasangæ, and the Asangæ,|| where tigers abound, noted for their ferocity. The force under arms consists of 30,000 foot, 300 elephants, and 800 horse. These are shut in by the Indus, and are surrounded by a circle of mountains and deserts

---

mouth of the Godâvari river. The town of *Dandaguda* or *Dandagula* I take to be the Dântapura of the Buddhist chronicles, which as the capital of Kalinga may with much probability be identified with Râja Mahendri, which is only 30 miles to the north-east of Coringa. From the great similarity of the Greek Γ and Π, I think it not improbable that the Greek name may have been *Dandapula*, which is almost the same as *Dântapura*. But in this case the *Dânta* or 'tooth-relic' of Buddha must have been enshrined in Kalinga as early as the time of Pliny, which is confirmed by the statement of the Buddhist chronicles that the 'left canine tooth' of Buddha was brought to Kalinga immediately after his death, where it was enshrined by the reigning sovereign, Brahmadatta."—Cunningham, *Geog.* p. 518.

‡ [Tropina answers to Tripontari or Tirupanatara, opposite Kochin.—Ed. *Ind. Ant.*] The distance given is measured from the mouth of the Ganges, and not from Cape Calingon.

§ This cape is a projecting point of the island of Perimula or Perimuda, now called the island of Salsette, near Bombay.

|| v. l. Asmagi. The Asangæ, as placed doubtfully by Lassen about Jodhpur.—Ed. *Ind. Ant.*

over a space of 625 miles.¶ Below the deserts are the Dari, the Suræ, then deserts again for 187 miles,* these deserts encircling the fertile tracts just as the sea encircles islands.† Below these deserts we find the Maltecoræ, Singhæ, Marohæ, Rarungæ, Moruni.‡ These inhabit the hills which in an unbroken

---

¶ *DCXXV.*—v. l. DCXXXV. Pliny, having given a general account of the basins of the Indus and the Ganges, proceeds to enumerate here the tribes which peopled the north of India. The names are obscure, but Lassen has identified one or two of them, and de Saint-Martin a considerable number more. The tribes first mentioned in the list occupied the country extending from the Jamunâ to the western coast about the mouth of the Narmadâ. The Cesi probably answer to the Khośas or Khasyas, a great tribe which from time immemorial has led a wandering life between Gujarât, the lower Indus, and the Jamunâ. The name of the Cetriboni would seem to be a transcript of Kêtrivani (for Kshatrivanêya). They may therefore have been a branch of the Kshatri (Khâtri), one of the impure tribes of the list of Manu (l. x. 12). The Megallæ must be identified with the Mâvelas of Sanskṛit books, a great tribe described as settled to the west of the Jamunâ. The Chrysei probably correspond to the Karoncha of the Purâṇic lists (*Vishṇu Pur.* pp. 177, 186, note 13, and 351, &c.). The locality occupied by these and the two tribes mentioned after them must have lain to the north of the Ran, between the lower Indus and the chain of the Arâvali mountains.

* *CLXXXVII.*—v. l. CLXXXVIII.

† The Dhârs inhabit still the banks of the lower Ghara and the parts contiguous to the valley of the Indus. Hiwen Thsâng mentions, however, a land of Dara at the lower end of the gulf of Kachh, in a position which quite accords with that which Pliny assigns to them. The Suræ, Sansk. Śûra, have their name preserved in "Saur," which designates a tribe settled along the Lower Indus—the modern representatives of the Saurabhîra of the *Harivaṁśa.* They are placed with doubt by Lassen on the Lonî about Sindri, but Yule places the Bolingæ—Sanskṛit, Bhaulingas—there.—Ed. *Ind. Ant.*

‡ *Moruni, &c.*—v. l. Moruntes, Masuæ Pagungæ, Lalii.

chain run parallel to the shores of the ocean. They are free and have no kings, and occupy the mountain heights, whereon they have built many cities.§ Next follow the N a r e æ, enclosed by the loftiest of Indian mountains, C a p i t a l i a.||

§ These tribes must have been located in Kachh, a mountainous tongue of land between the gulf of that name and the Raṇ, where, and where only, in this region of India, a range of mountains is to be found running along the coast. The name of the Maltecoræ has attracted particular attention because of its resemblance to the name of the Martikhora (*i. e.* man-eater), a fabulous animal mentioned by Ktêsias (*Ctesiæ Indica*, VII.) as found in India and subsisting upon human flesh. The Maltecoræ were consequently supposed to have been a race of cannibals. The identification is, however, rejected by M. de St.-Martin. The Singhæ are represented at the present day by the Sânghis of Omarkoṭ (called the Song by MacMurdo), descendants of an ancient Râjput tribe called the Singhârs. The Marohæ are probably the Maruhas of the list of the *Varâha Sanhitâ*, which was later than Pliny's time by four and a half centuries. In the interval they were displaced, but the displacement of tribes was nothing unusual in those days. So the Rarungæ may perhaps be the ancestors of the Ronghi or Rhanga now found on the banks of the Satlej and in the neighbourhood of Dihli.

|| Capitalia is beyond doubt the sacred Arbuda, or Mount Âbû, which, attaining an elevation of 6500 feet, rises far above any other summit of the Arâvali range. The name of the Naresæ recalls that of the Naïr, which the Râjput chroniclers apply to the northern belt of the desert (Tod, *Râjasthân*, II. 211); so St.-Martin; but according to General Cunningham they must be the people of Sarui, or 'the country of reeds, as *nar* and *sar* are synonymous terms for 'a reed,' and the country of Sarui is still famous for its reed-arrows. The same author uses the statement that extensive gold and silver mines were worked on the other side of Mount Capitalia in support of his theory that this part of India was the Ophir of Scripture, from which the Tyrian navy in the days of Solomon carried away gold, a great plenty of almug-trees (red sandalwood), and precious stones (1 Kings xii.). His argument runs thus:—" The last name in Pliny's list is Varetatæ, which I would change to Vataretæ by the transposition of two letters. This spelling is countenanced by the termination of the various read-

The inhabitants on the other side of this mountain work extensive mines of gold and silver. Next are the O r a t u r æ, whose king has only ten elephants, though he has a very strong force of in-

---

ing of Svarataratæ, which is found in some editions. It is quite possible, however, that the Svarataratæ may be intended for the Surâshṭras. The famous Varâha Mihira mentions the Surâshṭras and Bâdaras together, amongst the people of the south-west of India (Dr. Kern's *Bṛihat Sañhitâ*, XIV. 19.) These Bâdaras must therefore be the people of Badari, or Vaḍari. I understand the name of Vaḍari to denote a district abounding in the *Badari*, or *Ber*-tree (Jujube), which is very common in Southern Râjputânâ. For the same reason I should look to this neighbourhood for the ancient Sauvîra, which I take to be the true form of the famous Sophir, or Ophir, as Sauvîra is only another name of the Vaḍari or *Ber*-tree, as well as of its juicy fruit. Now, Sofir is the Coptic name of India at the present day; but the name must have belonged originally to that part of the Indian coast which was frequented by the merchants of the West. There can be little doubt, I think, that this was in the Gulf of Khambay, which from time immemorial has been the chief seat of Indian trade with the West. During the whole period of Greek history this trade was almost monopolized by the famous city of Barygaza, or Bhâroch, at the mouth of the Narmadâ river. About the fourth century some portion of it was diverted to the new capital of Balabhi, in the peninsula of Gujarât; in the Middle Ages it was shared with Khambay at the head of the gulf, and in modern times with Surat, at the mouth of the Tapti. If the name of Sauvîra was derived, as I suppose, from the prevalence of the Ber-tree, it is probable that it was only another appellation for the province of Badari, or Edar, at the head of the Gulf of Khambay. This, indeed, is the very position in which we should expect to find it, according to the ancient inscription of Rudra Dâma, which mentions Sindhu-Sauvîra immediately after Surâshṭra and Bhârukachha, and just before Kukura Aparanta, and Nishada (*Jour. Bo. Br. R. As. Soc.* VII. 120). According to this arrangement Sauvîra must have been to the north of Surâshṭra and Bhâroch, and to the south of Nishada, or just where I have placed it, in the neighbourhood of Mount Âbû. Much the same locality is assigned to Sauvîra in the *Vishnu Purâna.*" —*Anc. Geog. of Ind.* pp. 496-497 : see also pp. 560-562 of the same work, where the subject is further discussed.

fantry.¶ Next again are the V a r e t a t æ,* subject to a king, who keep no elephants, but trust entirely to their horse and foot. Then the O d o m b œ r æ; the S a l a b a s t r æ;† the H o r a t æ,‡ who have a fine city, defended by marshes which serve as a ditch, wherein crocodiles are kept, which, having a great avidity for human flesh, prevent all access to the city except by a bridge. And another city

---

¶ v. l. Oratæ. The Oraturæ find their representatives in the Râṭhors, who played a great part in the history of India before the Musulmân conquest, and who, though settled in the Gangetic provinces, regard Ajmir, at the eastern point of the Arâvalî, as their ancestral seat.

* v. l. Suarataratæ. The Varetatæ cannot with certainty be identified.

† The Odombœræ, with hardly a change in the form of their name, are mentioned in Sanskṛit literature, for Pâṇini (IV. 1, 173, quoted by Lassen, *Ind. Alt.* 1st ed. I. p. 614) speaks of the territory of Udumbari as that which was occupied by a tribe famous in the old legend, the Salva, who perhaps correspond to the Salabastræ of Pliny, the addition which he has made to their name being explained by the Sanskṛit word *vastya*, which means *an abode* or *habitation*. The word *udumbara* means the glomerous fig-tree. The district so named lay in Kachh. [The Salabastræ are located by Lassen between the mouth of the Sarasvatî and Jodhpur, and the Horatæ at the head of the gulf of Khambhât; Automela he places at Khambhât. See *Ind. Alterth.* 2nd ed. I. 760. Yule has the Sandrabatis about Chandrâvati, in northern Gujarât, but these are placed by Lassen on the Banâs about Tonk.—Ed. *Ind. Ant.*]

‡ *Horatæ* is an incorrect transcription of Soraṭh, the vulgar form of the Sanskṛit *Saurâshṭra*. The Horatæ were therefore the inhabitants of the region called in the *Periplûs*, and in Ptolemy, Surastrênê—that is, Gujarât. Orrhoth (Ὀῤῥοθα) is used by Kosmas as the name of a city in the west of India, which has been conjectured to be Surat, but Yule thinks it rather some place on the Purbandar coast. The capital, Automela, cannot be identified, but de St.-Martin conjectures it may have been the once famous Valabhî, which was situated in the peninsular part of Gujarât at about 24 miles' distance from the Gulf of Khambay.

of theirs is much admired—A u t o m e l a,§ which, being seated on the coast at the confluence of five rivers, is a noble emporium of trade. The king is master of 1600 elephants, 150,000 foot, and 5000 cavalry. The poorer king of the C h a r m æ has but sixty elephants, and his force otherwise is insignificant. Next come the P a n d æ, the only race in India ruled by women.|| They say that Hercules having but one daughter, who was on that account all the more beloved, endowed her with a noble kingdom. Her descendants rule over 300 cities, and command an army of 150,000 foot and 500 elephants. Next, with 300 cities, the S y r i e n i, D e r a n g æ, P o s i n g æ, B u z æ, G o g i a r e i, U m b r æ, N e r e æ, B r a n c o s i, N o b u n d æ, C o c o n d æ, N e s e i, P e d a t r i r æ, S o l o b r i a s æ, O l o s t r æ,¶ who adjoin the island Patale, from the

§ v. l. Automula. See preceding note.

|| The Charmæ have been identified with the inhabitants of Charmamandala, a district of the west mentioned in the *Mahâbhârata* and also in the *Vishṇu Purâṇa* under the form Charmakhanda. They are now represented by the Charmârs or Chamârs of Bundelkhand and the parts adjacent to the basin of the Ganges. The Pandæ, who were their next neighbours, must have occupied a considerable portion of the basin of the river Chambal, called in Sanskṛit geography the Charmanvatî. They were a branch of the famous race of Pâṇḍu, which made for itself kingdoms in several different parts of India.

¶ The names in this list lead us to the desert lying between the Indus and the Arâvalî range. Most of the tribes enumerated are mentioned in the lists of the clans given in the Râjput chronicles, and have been identified by M. de St.-Martin as follows :—The Syrieni are the Suriyanis, who under that name have at all times occupied the country near the Indus in the neighbourhood of Bakkar.

furthest shore of which to the Caspian gates the distance is said to be 1925 miles.*

Then next to these towards the Indus come, in an order which is easy to follow, the Amatæ, Bolingæ, Gallitalutæ, Dimuri, Megari, Ordabæ,† Mesæ; after these the Uri and Sileni.‡ Immediately beyond come

---

Darangæ is the Latin transcription of the name of the great race of the Jhâḍejâs, a branch of the Râjputs which at the present day possesses Kachh. The Buzæ represent the Buddas, an ancient branch of the same Jhâḍejâs (Tod, *Annals and Antiq, of the Râj.* vol. I. p. 86). The Gogiarei (other readings Gogarasi, Gogaræ) are the Kokaris, who are now settled on the banks of the Ghara or Lower Satlej. The Umbræ are represented by the Umranîs, and the Nerei perhaps by the Nharonis, who, though belonging to Baluchistân, had their ancestral seats in the regions to the east of the Indus. The Nubêteh, who figure in the old local traditions of Sindh, perhaps correspond to the Nobundæ, while the Cocondæ certainly are the Kokonadas mentioned in the *Mahâbhârata* among the people of the north-west. (See Lassen, *Zeitschrift für die Kunde des Morgenl.* t. II. 1839, p. 45.) Buchanan mentions a tribe called *Kakand* as belonging to Gorakhpur.

* There were two defiles, which went by the name of 'the Kaspian Gates.' One was in Albania, and was formed by the jutting out of a spur of the Kaukasos into the Kaspian Sea. The other, to which Pliny here refers, was a narrow pass leading from North-Western Asia into the north-east provinces of Persia. According to Arrian (*Anab.* III. 20) the Kaspian Gates lay a few days' journey distant from the Median town of Rhagai, now represented by the ruins called Rha, found a mile or two to the south of Teherân. This pass was one of the most important places in ancient geography, and from it many of the meridians were measured. Strabo, who frequently mentions it, states that its distance from the extreme promontories of India (Cape Comorin, &c.) was 14,000 stadia.

† v. l. Ardabæ.

‡ In the grammatical apophthegms of Pâṇini, Bhaulingi is mentioned as a territory occupied by a branch of the great tribe of the Śâlvas (Lassen, *Ind. Alt.* I. p. 613, note, or 2nd ed. p. 760 n.), and from this indication M. de St.-Martin has been led to place the Bolingæ at the western

deserts extending for 250 miles. These being passed, we come to the Organagæ, Abaortæ, Sibaræ, Suertæ, and after these to deserts as extensive as the former. Then come the Sarophages, Sorgæ, Baraomatæ, and the Umbrittæ,§ who consist of twelve tribes, each possessing two cities, and the Aseni, who possess three cities.|| Their capital is Bucephala, built where Alexander's famous horse

---

declivity of the Arâvalî mountains, where Ptolemy also places his Bolingæ. The Madrabhujingha of the Panjâb (see *Vishṇu Pur.* p. 187) were probably a branch of this tribe. The Gallitalutæ are identified by the same author with the Gahalata or Gehlots ; the Dimuri with the Dumras, who, though belonging to the Gangetic valley, originally came from that of the Indus ; the Megari with the Mokars of the Râjput chronicles, whose name is perhaps preserved in that of the Mehars of the lower part of Sindh, and also in that of the Meghâris of Eastern Baluchistân ; the Messæ with the Mazaris, a considerable tribe between Shikârpûr and Mitankôt on the western bank of the Indus ; and the Uri with the Hauras of the same locality —the Hurairas who figure in the Râjput lists of thirty-six royal tribes. The Sulalas of the same tribes perhaps represent the Sileni, whom Pliny mentions along with the Uri.

§ vv. ll. Paragomatæ, Umbitræ.—Baraomatæ Gumbritæque.

|| The tribes here enumerated must have occupied a tract of country lying above the confluence of the Indus with the stream of the combined rivers of the Panjâb. They are obscure, and their names cannot with any certainty be identified if we except that of the Sibaræ, who are undoubtedly the Sauvîras of the *Mahâbhârata*, and who, as their name is almost invariably combined with that of the Indus, must have dwelt not far from its banks. The Afghân tribe of the Afridîs may perhaps represent the Abaortæ, and the Sarabhân or Sarvanîs, of the same stock, the Sarophages. The Umbrittæ and the Aseni take us to the east of the river. The former are perhaps identical with the Ambastæ of the historians of Alexander, and the Ambasthas of Sanskṛit writings, who dwelt in the neighbourhood of the lower Akesinês.

of that name was buried.¶ Hillmen follow next, inhabiting the base of Caucasus, the Soleadæ, and the Sondræ; and if we cross to the other side of the Indus and follow its course downward we meet the Samarabriæ, Sambruceni, Bisambritæ,* Osii, Antixeni, and the Taxillæ† with a famous city. Then succeeds

---

¶ Alexander, after the great battle on the banks of the Hydaspês in which he defeated Pôros, founded two cities—Bukephala or Bukephalia, so named in honour of his celebrated charger, and Nikaia, so named in honour of his victory. Nikaia, it is known for certain, was built on the field of battle, and its position was therefore on the left side of the Hydaspês—probably about where Mong now stands. The site of Bukephala it is not so easy to determine. According to Plutarch and Pliny it was near the Hydaspês, in the place where Bukephalos was buried, and if that be so it must have been on the same side of the river as the sister city; whereas Strabo and all the other ancient authorities place it on the opposite side. Strabo again places it at the point where Alexander crossed the river, whereas Arrian states that it was built on the site of his camp. General Cunningham fixes this at Jalâlpur rather than at Jhelam, 30 miles higher up the river, the site which is favoured by Burnes and General Court and General Abbott. Jalâlpur is about ten miles distant from Dilâwar, where, according to Cunningham, the crossing of the river was most probably effected.

* v. l. Bisabritæ.

† The Soleadæ and the Sondræ cannot be identified, and of the tribes which were seated to the east of the Indus only the Taxillæ are known. Their capital was the famous Taxila, which was visited by Alexander the Great. "The position of this city," says Cunningham, "has hitherto remained unknown, partly owing to the erroneous distance recorded by Pliny, and partly to the want of information regarding the vast ruins which still exist in the vicinity of Shâh-dheri. All the copies of Pliny agree in stating that Taxila was only 60 Roman, or 55 English, miles from Peucolaïtis or Hashtnagar, which would fix its site somewhere on the Haro river to the west of Hasan Abdâl, or just two days' march from the Indus. But the itineraries of the Chinese pilgrims agree in placing it at three days' journey to the east of the Indus, or in the immediate neighbourhood of Kâla-ka-Sarâi. He therefore fixes its site near Shâh-dheri

a level tract of country known by the general name of Amanda,‡ whereof the tribes are four in number—the Peucolaitæ,§ Arsagalitæ, Geretæ, Asoi.

Many writers, however, do not give the river Indus as the western boundary of India, but include within it four satrapies,—the Gedrosi, Arachotæ, Arii, Paropamisadæ,||

(which is a mile to the north-east of that Sarâi), in the extensive ruins of a fortified city abounding with *stûpas*, monasteries, and temples. From this place to Hashtnagar the distance is 74 miles English, or 19 in excess of Pliny's estimate. Taxila represents the Sanskṛit Takshaśila, of which the Pali form is Takhasila, whence the Greek form was taken. The word means either 'cut rock' or 'severed head.'—*Anc. Geog. of Ind.* pp. 104-121.

‡ As the name Amanda is entirely unknown, M. de St.-Martin proposes without hesitation the correction Gandhâra, on the ground that the territory assigned to the Amanda corresponds exactly to Gandhâra, of which the territory occupied by the Peucolitæ (Peukelaôtis), as we know from other writers, formed a part. The Geretæ are beyond doubt no others than the Gouræi of Arrian; and the Asoi may perhaps be identical with the Aspasii, or, as Strabo gives the name, Hippasii or Pasii. The Arsagalitæ are only mentioned by Pliny. Two tribes settled in the same locality are perhaps indicated by the name—the Arsa, mentioned by Ptolemy, answering to the Sanskṛit Uraśa; and the Ghilit or Ghilghit, the Gahalata of Sanskṛit, formerly mentioned.

§ v. l. Peucolitæ.

|| Gedrôsia comprehended probably nearly the same district which is now known by the name of Mekrân. Alexander marched through it on returning from his Indian expedition. Arachôsia extended from the chain of mountains now called the Suleimân as far southward as Gedrôsia. Its capital, Arachotos, was situated somewhere in the direction of Kandahâr, the name of which, it has been thought, preserves that of Gandhâra. According to Colonel Rawlinson the name of Arachôsia is derived from Harakhwati (Sanskṛit *Sarasvati*), and is preserved in the Arabic *Rakhaj*. It is, as has already been noticed, the Harauvatas of the Bisutun inscription. Âria denoted the country lying between Meshed and Herât; Âriâna, of which it formed a

making the river Cophes its furthest limit; though others prefer to consider all these as belonging to the Arii.

Many writers further include in India even the city Nysa and Mount Merus, sacred to Father Bacchus, whence the origin of the fable that he sprang from the thigh of Jupiter. They include also the Astacani,¶ in whose country the vine

part, and of which it is sometimes used as the equivalent, was a wider district, which comprehended nearly the whole of ancient Persia. In the Persian part of the Bisutun inscription Âria appears as Hariva, in the Babylonian part as Arevan. Regarding Paropamisos and the Cophes see *Ind. Ant.* vol. V. pp. 329 and 330.

¶ Other readings of the name are Aspagani and Aspagonæ. M. de St.-Martin, whose work has so often been referred to, says:—"We have seen already that in an extract from old Hekataios preserved in Stephen of Byzantium the city of Kaspapyros is called a Gandaric city, and that in Herodotos the same place is attributed to the Paktyi, and we have added that in our opinion there is only an apparent contradiction, because the district of Paktyikê and Gandara may very well be but one and the same country. It is not difficult, in fact, to recognize in the designation mentioned by Herodotos the indigenous name of the Afghân people, Pakhtu (in the plural Pakhtûn), the name which the greater part of the tribes use among themselves, and the only one they apply to their national dialect. We have here, then, as Lassen has noticed, historical proof of the presence of the Afghâns in their actual fatherland five centuries at least before the Christian era. Now, as the seat of the Afghân or Pakht nationality is chiefly in the basin of the Kophês, to the west of the Indus, which forms its eastern boundary, this further confirms what we have already seen, that it is to the west of the great river we must seek for the site of the city of Kaspapyros or Kaśyapapura, and consequently of the Gandariê of Hekataios. The employment of two different names to designate the very same country is easily explained by this double fact, that one of the names was the Indian designation of the land, whilst the other was the indigenous name applied to it by its inhabitants. There was yet another name, of Sanskṛit origin, used as a territorial appellation of Gandhâra—that of Aśvaka. This word,

grows abundantly, and the laurel, and boxwood, and every kind of fruit-tree found in Greece. The remarkable and almost fabulous accounts which are current regarding the fertility of its soil, and the nature of its fruits and trees, its beasts and birds and other animals, will be set down each in its own place in other parts of this work. A little further on I shall speak of the satrapies, but the island of T a p r o b a n e§ requires my immediate attention.

But before we come to this island there are others, one being P a t a l e, which, as we have indicated, lies at the mouth of the Indus, triangular in shape, and 220‖ miles in breadth. Beyond the mouth of the Indus are C h r y s e and A r g y r e,¶

---

derived from *aśva*, a horse, signified merely *the cavaliers*; it was less an ethnic, in the rigorous acceptation of the word, than a general appellation applied by the Indians of the Panjâb to the tribes of the region of the Kophês, renowned from antiquity for the excellence of its horses. In the popular dialects the Sanskṛit word took the usual form Assaka, which reappears scarcely modified in Assakani (Ἀσσακανοί) or Assakêni (Ἀσσακηνοί) in the Greek historians of the expedition of Alexander and subsequent writers. It is impossible not to recognize here the name of Avghân or Afghâns. . . which is very evidently nothing else than a contracted form of Assakân. . . Neither the Gandariê of Hekataios nor the Paktyi of Herodotos are known to them [Arrian and other Greek and Latin writers of the history of Alexander], but as it is the same territory [as that of the Assakani], and as in actual usage the names Afghâns and Pakhtûn are still synonymous, their identity is not a matter of doubt."—*E'tude sur le Géographie Grecque et Latine de l'Inde*, pp. 376-8. The name of the Gandhâra, it may here be added, remounts to the highest antiquity; it is mentioned in one of the hymns of the Rig-Veda, as old perhaps as the 15th century B.C.—*Id.* p. 864.

§ *Vide ante*, p. 62, n. *. ‖ CCXX.—v. l. CXXX.

¶ Burma and Arakan respectively, according to Yule.—Ed. *Ind. Ant.*

rich, as I believe, in metals. For I cannot readily believe, what is asserted by some writers, that their soil is impregnated with gold and silver. At a distance of twenty miles from these lies Crocala,* from which, at a distance of twelve miles, is Bibaga, which abounds with oysters and other shell-fish.† Next comes Toralliba,‡ nine miles distant from the last-named island, beside many others unworthy of note.

FRAGM. LVI. B.

Solin. 52. 6-17.

Catalogue of Indian Races.

The greatest rivers of India are the Ganges and Indus, and of these some assert that the Ganges rises from uncertain sources and inundates the country in the manner of the Nile, while others incline to think that it rises in the Scythian mountains. [The Hypanis is also there, a very noble river, which formed the limit of Alexander's march, as the altars erected *on its banks* prove.§]

---

* In the bay of Karâchi, identical with the Kolaka of Ptolemy. The district in which Karâchî is situated is called Karkalla to this day.

† This is called Bibakta by Arrian, *Indika*, cap. xxi.

‡ v. l. Coralliba.

§ See Arrian's *Anab.* V. 29, where we read that Alexander having arranged his troops in separate divisions ordered them to build on the banks of the Hyphasis twelve altars to be of equal height with the loftiest towers, while exceeding them in breadth. From Curtius we learn that they were formed of square blocks of stone. There has been much controversy regarding their site, but it must have been near the capital of Sopithês, whose name Lassen has identified with the Sanskṛit *Aśvapati*, 'lord of

The least breadth of the Ganges is eight miles, and its greatest twenty. Its depth where it is shallowest is fully a hundred feet. The people who live in the furthest-off part are the G a n g a r i d e s, whose king possesses 1000 horse, 700 elephants, and 60,000 foot in apparatus of war.

Of the Indians some cultivate the soil, very many follow war, and others trade. The noblest and richest manage public affairs, administer justice, and sit in council with the kings. There exists also a fifth class, consisting of those most eminent for their wisdom, who, when sated with life, seek death by mounting a burning funeral pile. Those, however, who have become the devotees of a sterner sect, and pass their life in the woods, hunt elephants, which, when made quite tame and docile, they use for ploughing and for riding on.

In the Ganges there is an island extremely populous, occupied by a very powerful nation whose king keeps under arms 50,000 foot and 4000 horse. In fact no one invested with kingly power ever keeps on foot a military force without a very great number of elephants and foot and cavalry.

The P r a s i a n nation, which is extremely powerful, inhabits a city called P a l i b ô t r a, whence some call the nation itself the P a l i b ô t r i. Their

---

horses.' These Asvapati were a line of princes whose territory, according to the 12th book of the *Râmâyana*, lay on the right or north bank of the Vipâśa (Hyphasis or Biâs), in the mountainous part of the Doâb comprised between that river and the Upper Irâvati. Their capital is called in the poem of Vâlmiki Râjagriha, which still exists under the name of Râjagiri. At some distance from this there is a chain of heights called Sekandar-giri, or 'Alexander's mountain.'—See St.-Martin's *E'tude*, &c. pp. 108-111.

king keeps in his pay at all times 60,000 foot 30,000 horse, and 8000 elephants.

Beyond Palibôtra is Mount Maleus,|| on which shadows in winter fall towards the north, in summer towards the south, for six months alternately. In that region the Bears are seen but once a year, and not for more than fifteen days, as Beton informs us, who allows that this happens in many parts of India. Those living near the river Indus in the regions that turn southward are scorched more than others by the heat, and at last the complexion of the people is visibly affected by the great power of the sun. The mountains are inhabited by the Pygmies.

But those who live near the sea have no kings. The Pandæan nation is governed by females, and their first queen is said to have been the daughter of Hercules. The city Nysa is assigned to this region, as is also the mountain sacred to Jupiter, Mêros by name, in a cave on which the ancient Indians affirm Father Bacchus was nourished; while the name has given rise to the well-known fantastic story that Bacchus was born from the thigh of his father. Beyond the mouth of the Indus are two islands, Chryse and Argyre, which yield such an abundant supply of metals that many writers allege their soils consist of gold and of silver.

|| Possibly, as suggested by Yule, Mount Pârśvanâtha, near the Damudâ, and not far from the Tropic; *vide Ind. Ant.* vol. VI. p. 127, note §, and conf. vol. I. p. 46ff. The Malli (see above), in whose country it was, are not to be confounded with another tribe of the same name in the Panjâb, mentioned by Arrian; see vol. V. pp. 87, 96, 383.—Ed. *Ind. Ant.*

Fragm. LVII.

Polyæn. *Strateg.* I. 1. 1-3.

Of Dionysos.

(Cf. Epit. 25 *et seq.*)

Dionysos, in his expedition against the Indians, in order that the cities might receive him willingly, disguised the arms with which he had equipped his troops, and made them wear soft raiment and fawn-skins. The spears were wrapped round with ivy, and the thyrsus had a sharp point. He gave the signal for battle by cymbals and drums instead of the trumpet, and by regaling the enemy with wine diverted their thoughts from war to dancing. These and all other Bacchic orgies were employed in the system of warfare by which he subjugated the Indians and all the rest of Asia.

Dionysos, in the course of his Indian campaign, seeing that his army could not endure the fiery heat of the air, took forcible possession of the three-peaked mountain of India. Of these peaks one is called K o r a s i b i ê, another K o n d a s k ê, but to the third he himself gave the name of M ê r o s, in remembrance of his birth. Thereon were many fountains of water sweet to drink, game in great plenty, tree-fruits in unsparing profusion, and snows which gave new vigour to the frame. The troops quartered there made a sudden descent upon the barbarians of the plain, whom they easily routed, since they attacked them with missiles from a commanding position on the heights above.

[Dionysos, after conquering the Indians, invaded Baktria, taking with him as auxiliaries the Indians and Amazons. That country has for its boundary the river S a r a n g ê s.¶ The Baktrians seized the mountains overhanging that river with a view to attack Dionysos, in crossing it, from a post of advantage. He, however, having encamped along the river, ordered the Amazons and the Bakkhai to cross it, in order that the Baktrians, in their contempt for women, might be induced to come down from the heights. The women then assayed to cross the stream, and the enemy came downhill, and advancing to the river endeavoured to beat them back. The women then retreated, and the Baktrians pursued them as far as the bank ; then Dionysos, coming to the rescue with his men, slew the Baktrians, who were impeded from fighting by the current, and he crossed the river in safety.

Fragm. LVIII.

Polyæn. *Strateg*. I. 3. 4.

Of Hercules and Pandæa.

(Cf. Fragm. L. 15.)

H e r a k l ê s begat a daughter in India whom he called P a n d a i a. To her he assigned that portion of India which lies to southward and extends to the sea, while he distributed the people subject to her rule into 365 villages, giving orders that one village should each day bring to the

¶ See *Ind. Ant., Notes to Arrian* in vol. V. p. 332.

treasury the royal tribute, so that the queen might always have the assistance of those men whose turn it was to pay the tribute in coercing those who for the time being were defaulters in their payments.

Fragm. LIX.

Of the Beasts of India.

Ælian, *Hist. Anim.* XVI. 2-22.*

(2) In India I learn that there are to be found the birds *called* parrots; and though I have, no doubt, already mentioned them, yet what I omitted to state previously regarding them may now with great propriety be here set down. There are, I am informed, three species of them, and all these, if taught to speak, as children are taught, become as talkative as children, and speak with a human voice; but in the woods they utter a bird-like scream, and neither send out any distinct and musical notes, nor being wild and untaught are able to talk. There are also peacocks in India, the largest anywhere met with,

* "In this extract not a few passages occur which appear to have been borrowed from Megasthenês. This conjecture, though it cannot by any means be placed beyond doubt by conclusive proofs, seems nevertheless, for various reasons, to attain a certain degree of probability. For in the first place the author knows with unusual accuracy the interior parts of India. Then again he makes very frequent mention of the Prasii and the Brâhmaṇs. And lastly one can hardly doubt that some chapters occurring in the middle of this part have been extracted from Megasthenês. I have, therefore, in this uncertainty taken care that the whole of this part should be printed at the end of the fragments of Megasthenês."—Schwanbeck.

and pale-green ringdoves. One who is not well-versed in bird-lore, seeing these for the first time, would take them to be parrots, and not pigeons. In the colour of the bill and legs they resemble Greek partridges. There are also cocks, which are of extraordinary size, and have their crests not red as elsewhere, or at least in our country, but have the flower-like coronals *of which the crest is formed* variously coloured. Their rump feathers, again, are neither curved nor wreathed, but are of great breadth, and they trail them in the way peacocks trail their tails, when they neither straighten nor erect them: the feathers of these Indian cocks are in colour golden, and also dark-blue like the smaragdus.

(3) There is found in India also another *remarkable* bird. This is of the size of a starling and is parti-coloured, and is trained to utter the sounds of human speech. It is even more talkative than the parrot, and of greater natural cleverness. So far is it from submitting with pleasure to be fed by man, that it rather has such a pining for freedom, and such a longing to warble at will in the society of its mates, that it prefers starvation to slavery with sumptuous fare. It is called by the Makedonians who settled among the Indians in the city of Boukephala and its neighbourhood, and in the city called Kuropolis, and others which Alexander the son of Philip built, the *Kerkiôn*. This name had, I believe, its ori-

gin in the fact that the bird wags its tail in the same way as the water-ousels (οἱ κίγκλοι).

(4) I learn further that in India there is a bird called the *Kêlas*, which is thrice the size of the bustard, and has a bill of prodigious size and long legs. It is furnished also with an immense crop resembling a leather pouch. The cry which it utters is peculiarly discordant. The plumage is ash-coloured, except that the feathers at their tips are tinted with a pale yellow.

(5) I hear also that the Indian hoopoe (ἔποπα) is double the size of ours, and more beautiful in appearance, and Homer says that while the bridle and trappings of a horse are the delight of a Hellenic king, this hoopoe is the favourite plaything of the king of the Indians, who carries it on his hand, and toys with it, and never tires gazing in ecstasy on its splendour, and the beauty with which Nature has adorned it. The Brachmanes, therefore, even make this particular bird the subject of a mythic story, and the tale told of it runs thus :—To the king of the Indians there was born a son. The child had elder brothers, who when they came to man's estate turned out to be very unjust and the greatest of reprobates. They despised their brother because he was the youngest; and they scoffed also at their father and their mother, whom they despised because they were very old and grey-haired. The boy, accordingly, and his aged parents could at last no longer live with these wicked men, and away they fled from home, all

three together. In the course of the protracted journey which they had then to undergo, the old people succumbed to fatigue and died, and the boy showed them no light regard, but buried them in himself, having cut off his head with a sword. Then, as the Brachmanes tell us, the all-seeing sun, in admiration of this surpassing act of piety, transformed the boy into a bird which is most beautiful to behold, and which lives to a very advanced age. So on his head there grew up a crest which was, as it were, a memorial of what he had done at the time of his flight. The Athenians have also related, in a fable, marvels somewhat similar of the crested lark ; and this fable Aristophanes, the comic poet, appears to me to have followed when he says in the *Birds*, " For thou wert ignorant, and not always bustling, nor always thumbing Æsop, who spake of the crested lark, calling it the first of all birds, born before ever the earth was ; and telling how afterwards her father became sick and died, and how that, as the earth did not then exist, he lay unburied till the fifth day, when his daughter, unable to find a grave elsewhere, dug one for him in her own head."||

|| Lines 470-75 :—

" You're such a dull incurious lot, unread in Æsop's lore,
Whose story says the lark was born first of the feathered quire,
Before the earth ; then came a cold and carried off his sire :
Earth was not : five days lay the old bird untombed : at last the son
Buried the father in his head, since other grave was none."

Dr. Kennedy's translation.

It seems, accordingly, probable that the fable, though with a different bird for its subject, emanated from the Indians, and spread onward even to the Greeks. For the Brachmanes say that a prodigious time has elapsed since the Indian hoopoe, then in human form and young in years, performed that act of piety to its parents.

(6.) In India there is an animal closely resembling in appearance the land crocodile, and somewhere about the size of a little Maltese dog. It is covered all over with a scaly skin so rough altogether and compact that when flayed off it is used by the Indians as a file. It cuts through brass and eats iron. They call it the *phattages* (pangolin or scaly ant-eater) . . . .

(8.) The Indian sea breeds sea-snakes which have broad tails, and the lakes breed hydras of immense size, but these sea-snakes appear to inflict a bite more sharp than poisonous.

(9.) In India there are herds of wild horses, and also of wild asses. They say that the mares submit to be covered by the asses, and enjoy such coition, and breed mules, which are of a reddish colour and very fleet, but impatient of the yoke and otherwise skittish. They say that they catch these mules with foot-traps, and then take them to the king of the Prasians, and that if they are caught when two years old they do not refuse to be broken in, but if caught when beyond that age they differ in no respect from sharp-toothed and carnivorous animals.

(Fragm. XII. B follows here.)

(11.) There is found in India a graminivorous animal which is double the size of a horse, and which has a very bushy tail purely black in colour. The hair of this tail is finer than human hair, and its possession is a point on which Indian women set great store, for therewith they make a charming coiffure, by binding and braiding it with the locks of their own natural hair. The length of a hair is two cubits, and from a single root there sprout out, in the form of a fringe, somewhere about thirty hairs. The animal itself is the most timid that is known, for should it perceive that any one is looking at it, it starts off at its utmost speed, and runs right forward,—but its eagerness to escape is greater than the rapidity of its pace. It is hunted with horses and hounds good to run. When it sees that it is on the point of being caught, it hides its tail in some near thicket, while it stands at bay facing its pursuers, whom it watches narrowly. It even plucks up courage in a way, and thinks that since its tail is hid from view the hunters will not care to capture it, for it knows that its tail is the great object of attraction. But it finds this to be, of course, a vain delusion, for some one hits it with a poisoned dart, who then flays off the entire skin (for this is of value) and throws away the carcase, as the Indians make no use of any part of its flesh.

(12.) But further: whales are to be found

in the Indian Sea, and these five times larger than the largest elephant. A rib of this monstrous fish measures as much as twenty cubits, and its lip fifteen cubits. The fins near the gills are each of them so much as seven cubits in breadth. The shell-fish called *Kêrukes* are also met with, and the purple-fish of a size that would admit it easily into a gallon measure, while on the other hand the shell of the sea-urchin is large enough to cover completely a measure of that size. But fish in India attain enormous dimensions, especially the sea-wolves, the thunnies, and the golden-eyebrows. I hear also that at the season when the rivers are swollen, and with their full and boisterous flood deluge all the land, the fish are carried into the fields, where they swim and wander to and fro, even in shallow water, and that when the rains which flood the rivers cease, and the waters retiring from the land resume their natural channels, then in the low-lying tracts and in flat and marshy grounds, where we may be sure the so-called Nine are wont to have some watery recesses (κόλπους), fish even of eight cubits' length are found, which the husbandmen themselves catch as they swim about languidly on the surface of the water, which is no longer of a depth they can freely move in, but in fact so very shallow that it is with the utmost difficulty they can live in it at all.

(13.) The following fish are also indigenous

to India:—prickly roaches, which are never in any respect smaller than the asps of Argolis; and shrimps, which in India are even larger than crabs. These, I must mention, finding their way from the sea up the Ganges, have claws which are very large, and which feel rough to the touch. I have ascertained that those shrimps which pass from the Persian Gulf into the river Indus have their prickles smooth, and the feelers with which they are furnished elongated and curling, but this species has no claws.

(14.) The tortoise is found in India, where it lives in the rivers. It is of immense size, and it has a shell not smaller than a full-sized skiff (σκάφη), and which is capable of holding ten *medimni* (120 gallons) of pulse. There are, however, also land-tortoises which may be about as big as the largest clods turned up in a rich soil where the glebe is very yielding, and the plough sinks deep, and, cleaving the furrows with ease, piles the clods up high. These are said to cast their shell. Husbandmen, and all the hands engaged in field labour, turn them up with their mattocks, and take them out just in the way one extracts wood-worms from the plants they have eaten into. They are fat things and their flesh is sweet, having nothing of the sharp flavour of the sea-tortoise.

(15.) Intelligent animals are to be met with among ourselves, but they are few, and not at all so common as they are in India. For there we find the elephant, which answers to this character, and the parrot, and apes of the sphinx kind, and the creatures called satyrs. Nor must we forget the Indian ant, which is so noted for its wisdom. The ants of our own country do, no doubt, dig for themselves subterranean holes and burrows, and by boring provide themselves with lurking-places, and wear out all their strength in what may be called mining operations, which are indescribably toilsome and conducted with secrecy; but the Indian ants construct for themselves a cluster of tiny dwelling-houses, seated not on sloping or level grounds where they could easily be inundated, but on steep and lofty eminences. And in these, by boring out with untold skill certain circuitous passages which remind one of the Egyptian burial-vaults or Cretan labyrinths, they so contrive the structure of their houses that none of the lines run straight, and it is difficult for anything to enter them or flow into them, the windings and perforations being so tortuous. On the outside they leave only a single aperture to admit themselves and the grain which they collect and carry to their store-chambers. Their object in selecting lofty sites for their mansions is, of course, to escape the high floods and inundations of the rivers; and they derive this advantage from their foresight, that they live as it were in so many watch-towers or islands when the parts around the heights become all a lake. Moreover, the mounds they live in, though placed in contiguity, so far from being loosened and torn asunder by the deluge, are rather strengthened, especially by the morning dew: for they put on, so to speak, a coat of ice formed from this dew—thin, no doubt, but still of strength; while at the same time they are made more compact at their base by weeds and bark of trees adhering, which the silt of the river has carried down. Let so much about Indian ants be said by me now, as it was said by Iobas long ago.

(16) In the country of the Indian Areianoi there is a subterranean chasm down in which there are mysterious vaults, concealed ways, and thoroughfares invisible to men. These are deep withal, and stretch to a very great distance. How they came to exist, and how they were excavated, the Indians do not say, nor do I concern myself to inquire. Hither the Indians bring more than thrice ten thousand head of cattle of different kinds, sheep and goats, and oxen and horses; and every person who has been terrified by an ominous dream, or a warning sound or prophetic voice, or who has seen a bird of evil augury, as a substitute for his life casts into the chasm such a victim as his private means can afford, giving the animal as a ransom to save his soul alive. The victims conducted thither are not led in chains nor otherwise coerced, but they go along this road willingly, as if urged forward by some mysterious spell; and as soon as they find themselves on the verge

of the chasm they voluntarily leap in, and disappear for ever from human sight so soon as they fall into this mysterious and viewless cavern of the earth. But above there are heard the bellowings of oxen, the bleating of sheep, the neighing of horses, and the plaintive cries of goats, and if any one goes near enough to the edge and closely applies his ear he will hear afar off the sounds just mentioned. This commingled sound is one that never ceases, for every day that passes men bring new victims to be their substitutes. Whether the cries of the animals last brought only are heard, or the cries also of those brought before, I know not,—all I know is that the cries are heard.

(17) In the sea which has been mentioned they say there is a very large island, of which, as I hear, the name is T a p r o b a n ê. From what I can learn, it appears to be a very long and mountainous island, having a length of 7000 stadia and a breadth of 5000.¶ It has not, however, any cities, but only villages, of which the number amounts to 750. The houses in which the inhabitants lodge themselves are made of wood, and sometimes also of reeds.

(18.) In the sea which surrounds the islands, tortoises are bred of so vast a size that their shells are employed to make roofs for the houses: for a shell, being fifteen cubits in length, can hold a

¶ In the classical writers the size of this island is always greatly exaggerated. Its actual length from north to south is 271½ miles, and its breadth from east to west 137½, and its circuit about 650 miles.

good many people under it, screening them from the scorching heat of the sun, besides affording them a welcome shade. But, more than this, it is a protection against the violence of storms of rain far more effective than tiles, for it at once shakes off the rain that dashes against it, while those under its shelter hear the rain rattling as on the roof of a house. At all events they do not require to shift their abode, like those whose tiling is shattered, for the shell is hard and like a hollowed rock and the vaulted roof of a natural cavern.

The island, then, in the great sea, which they call Taprobanê, has palm-groves, where the trees are planted with wonderful regularity all in a row, in the way we see the keepers of pleasure-parks plant out shady trees in the choicest spots. It has also herds of elephants, which are there very numerous and of the largest size. These island elephants are more powerful than those of the mainland, and in appearance larger, and may be pronounced to be in every possible way more intelligent. The islanders export them to the mainland opposite in boats, which they construct expressly for this traffic from wood supplied by the thickets of the island, and they dispose of their cargoes to the king of the Kalingai. On account of the great size of the island, the inhabitants of the interior have never seen the sea, but pass their lives as if resident on a continent, though no doubt they learn from others that they are all around enclosed by the sea. The inhabitants, again, of the coast have no practical acquaintance with elephant-catching, and know of it only by report. All their energy is devoted to catching fish and the monsters of the deep; for the sea encircling the island is reported to breed an incredible number of fish, both of the smaller fry and of the monstrous sort, among the latter being some which have the heads of lions and of panthers and of other wild beasts, and also of rams; and, what is still a greater marvel, there are monsters which in all points of their shape resemble satyrs. Others are in appearance like women, but, instead of having locks of hair, are furnished with prickles. It is even solemnly alleged that this sea contains certain strangely formed creatures, to represent which in a picture would baffle all the skill of the artists of the country, even though, with a view to make a profound sensation, they are wont to paint monsters which consist of different parts of different animals pieced together. These have their tails and the parts which are wreathed of great length, and have for feet either claws or fins. I learn further that they are amphibious, and by night graze on the pasture-fields, for they eat grass like cattle and birds that pick up seeds. They have also a great liking for the date when ripe enough to drop from the palms, and accordingly they twist their coils, which are supple, and large enough for the purpose, around these trees, and shake them so violently that the dates come tumbling down, and afford them a welcome repast. Thereafter when the night begins gradually to wane, but before there is yet clear daylight, they disappear by plunging into the sea just as the first flush of morning faintly illumines its surface. They say whales also frequent this sea, though it is not true that they come near the shore lying in wait for thunnies. The dolphins are reported to be of two sorts—one fierce and armed with sharp-pointed teeth, which gives endless trouble to the fisherman, and is of a remorselessly cruel disposition, while the other kind is naturally mild and tame, swims about in the friskiest way, and is quite like a fawning dog. It does not run away when any one tries to stroke it, and it takes with pleasure any food it is offered.

(19.) The sea-hare, by which I now mean the kind found in the great sea (for of the kind found in the other sea I have already spoken), resembles in every particular the land hare except only the fur, which in the case of the land animal is soft and lies smoothly down, and does not resist the touch, whereas its brother of the sea has bristling hair which is prickly, and inflicts a wound on any one who touches it. It is said to swim atop of the sea-ripple without ever diving below, and to be very rapid in its movements. To catch it alive is no easy matter, as it never falls into the net, nor goes near the line and bait of the fishing-rod. When it suffers, however, from disease, and, being in consequence hardly able to swim, is cast out on shore, then if any one touches it with his hand death ensues if he is not attended to,—nay, should one, were it only with a staff, touch this dead hare, he is affected in the same way as those who have touched a basilisk. But a root, it is said, grows along the coast of the island, well known to every one, which is a remedy for the swooning which ensues. It is brought close to the nostrils of the person who has fainted, who thereupon recovers consciousness. But should the remedy not be applied the injury proves fatal to life, so noxious is the vigour which this hare has at its command.

Frag. XV. B. follows here.*

(22.) There is also a race called the S k i r a t a i,† whose country is beyond India. They are

---

* This is the fragment in which Ælian describes the one-horned animal which he calls the Kartazôn. Rosenmüller, who has treated at large of the unicorn, which he identifies with the Indian rhinoceros, thinks that Ælian probably borrowed his account of it from Ktêsias, who when in Persia may have heard exaggerated accounts of it, or may have seen it represented in sculpture with variations from its actual appearance. Tychsen derives its name from *Kerd,* an old name, he says, of the rhinoceros itself, and *tazan, i.e., currens velox, irruens.* Three animals were spoken of by the ancients as having a single horn—the African Oryx, the Indian Ass, and what is specially called the Unicorn. *Vide ante,* p. 59.

† *Vide ante,* Fragm. xxx. 3, p. 80, and p. 74, note †, where they are identified with the Kirâtas. In the *Râmâyana* there is a passage quoted by Lassen (*Zeitschr. f. Kunde d. Morgenl.* II. 40) where are mentioned "the Kirâtas, some of whom dwell in Mount Mandara, others use their ears as a covering; they are horrible, black-faced, with but one foot

snub-nosed, either because in the tender years of infancy their nostrils are pressed down, and continue to be so throughout their after-life, or because such is the natural shape of the organ. Serpents of enormous size are bred in their country, of which some kinds seize the cattle when at pasture and devour them, while other kinds only suck the blood, as do the *Aigithelai* in Greece, of which I have already spoken in the proper place.

---

but very fleet, who cannot be exterminated, are brave men, and cannibals." (Schwanbeck, p. 66.) [Lassen places one branch of them on the south bank of the Kausî in Nipâl, and another in Tiperâ.—Ed. *Ind. Ant.*]

TRANSLATION

OF THE

FIRST PART OF THE INDIKA OF ARRIAN.

CHAPS. I.—XVII. INCLUSIVE.

FROM TEUBNER'S EDITION,
LEIPZIG, 1867.

INTRODUCTION.

ARRIAN, who variously distinguished himself as a philosopher, a statesman, a soldier, and an historian, was born in Nikomedia, in Bithynia, towards the end of the first century. He became a pupil of the philosopher Epiktêtos, whose lectures he published. Having been appointed prefect of Kappadokia under the emperor Hadrian, he acquired during his administration a practical knowledge of the tactics of war in repelling an attack made upon his province by the Alani and Massagetæ. His talents recommended him to the favour of the succeeding emperor, Antoninus Pius, by whom he was raised to the consulship (A.D. 146). In his later years he retired to his native town, where he applied his leisure to the composition of works on history, to which he was led by his admiration of Xenophon. He died at an advanced age, in the reign of the emperor Marcus Aurelius. The work by which he is best known is his account of the Asiatic expedition of Alexander the Great, which is remarkable alike for the accuracy of its narrative, and the Xenophontic ease and clearness, if not the perfect purity, of its style. His work on India (Ἰνδική or τὰ Ἰνδικά) may be regarded as a continuation of his *Anabasis*, though it is not written, like the *Anabasis*, in the Attic dialect, but in the Ionic. The reason may have been that he

W

wished his work to supersede the old and less accurate account of India written in Ionic by Ktêsias of Knidos.

The *Indika* consists of three parts:—the first gives a general description of India, based chiefly on the accounts of the country given by Megasthenês and Eratosthenês (chaps. i.—xvii.); the second gives an account of the voyage made by Nearchos the Kretan from the Indus to the Pasitigris, based entirely on the narrative of the voyage written by Nearchos himself (chaps. xviii.—xlii.); the third contains a collection of proofs to show that the southern parts of the world are uninhabitable on account of the great heat (chap. xlii. to the end).

THE INDIKA OF ARRIAN.

I. The regions beyond the river Indus on the west are inhabited, up to the river Kôphen, by two Indian tribes, the Astakenoi and the Assakenoi, who are not men of great stature like the Indians on the other side of the Indus, nor so brave, nor yet so swarthy as most Indians. They were in old times subject to the Assyrians, then after a period of Median rule submitted to the Persians, and paid to Kyros the son of Kambysês the tribute from their land which Kyros had imposed. The Nysaioi, however, are not an Indian race, but descendants of those who came into India with Dionysos,—perhaps not only of those Greeks who had been disabled for service in the course of the wars which Dionysos waged against the Indians, but perhaps also of natives of the country whom Dionysos, with their own consent, had settled along with the Greeks. The district in which he planted this colony he named Nysaia, after Mount Nysa, and the city itself Nysa.* But the mountain

* Nysa, the birthplace of the wine-god, was placed, according to fancy, anywhere up and down the world wherever the vine was found to flourish. Now, as the region watered by the Kôphês was in no ordinary measure feracious of the joyous tree, there was consequently a Nysa somewhere upon its banks. Lassen doubted whether there

close by the city, and on the lower slopes of which it is built, is designated M ê r o s, from the accident which befell the god immediately after his birth. These stories about Dionysos are of course but fictions of the poets, and we leave them to the learned among the Greeks or barbarians to explain as they may. In the dominions of the A s s a k e n o i there is a great city called M a s s a k a, the seat of the sovereign power which controls the whole realm.† And there is another city, P e u k e l a ï t i s, which is also of great size and not far from the Indus.‡ These

---

was a city to the name; but M. de St.-Martin is less sceptical, and would identify it with an existing village which preserves traces of its name, being called Nysatta. This, he says, is near the northern bank of the river of Kabûl at less than two leagues below Hashṭnagar, and may suitably represent the Nysa of the historians. This place, he adds, ought to be of Median or Persian foundation, since the nomenclature is Irânian, the name of Nysa or Niśaya which figures in the cosmogonic geography of the *Zendavesta* being one which is far-spread in the countries of ancient Irân. He refers his readers for remarks on this point to A. de Humboldt's *Central Asia*, I. pp. 116 *seq*. ed. 1843.

† M a s s a k a (other forms are Massaga, Masaga, and Mazaga.)—The Sanskṛit M a ś a k â, a city situated near the Gauri. Curtius states that it was defended by a rapid river on its eastern side. When attacked by Alexander, it held out for four days against all his assaults.

‡ P e u k e l a ï t i s (other forms—Peukelaëtis, Peukolitæ, Peukelaötis). "The Greek name of Peukelaotis or Peukolaitis was immediately derived from Pukkalaoti, which is the Pâli or spoken form of the Sanskṛit P u s h k a l a v a t i. It is also called P e u k e l a s by Arrian, and the people are named P e u k a l e i by Dionysius Periegetes, which are both close transcripts of the Pâli P u k k a l a. The form of Proklaïs, which is found in Arrian's *Periplus of the Erythræan Sea* and also in Ptolemy's *Geography*, is perhaps only an attempt to give the Hindi name of P o k h a r, instead of the Sanskṛit P u s h k a r a." So General Cunningham, who fixes its position at "the two large towns

settlements lie on the other side of the river Indus, and extend in a westward direction as far as the K ô p h e n.

II. Now the countries which lie to the east of the Indus I take to be I n d i a Proper, and the people who inhabit them to be I n d i a n s.§ The northern boundaries of India *so defined* are formed by Mount T a u r o s, though the range does not retain that name in these parts. Tauros begins from the sea which washes the coasts of Pamphylia, Lykia, and Kilikia, and stretches away towards the Eastern Sea, intersecting the whole continent of Asia. The range bears different names in the different countries which it traverses. In one place it is called P a r a p a m i s o s, in another E m o d o s,|| and in a

---

Parāng and Chârsada, which form part of the well-known H a s h ṭ n a g a r, or 'eight cities,' that are seated close together on the eastern bank of the lower Swât river." The position indicated is nearly seventeen miles to the north-east of Peshâwar. P u s h k â l a, according to Prof. Wilson, is still represented by the modern P e k h e l y or Pakholi, in the neighbourhood of Peshâwar.

§ In limiting India to the eastern side of the Indus, Arrian expresses the view generally held in antiquity, which would appear to be also that of the Hindus themselves, since they are forbidden by one of their old traditions to cross that river. Much, however, may be said for the theory which would extend India to the foot of the great mountain ranges of Hindu Kush and Parapamisos. There is, for instance, the fact that in the region lying between these mountains and the Indus many places either now bear, or have formerly borne, names which can with certainty be traced to Sanskṛit sources. The subject is discussed at some length in Elphinstone's *History of India*, pp. 331-6, also by de St.-Martin.—*E'tude*, pp. 9-14.

|| P a r a p a m i s o s (other forms—Paropamisos, Paropamissos, Paropanisos). This denotes the great mountain range now called H i n d û K u s h, supposed to

third I m a o s, and it has perhaps other names besides. The Makedonians, again, who served with Alexander called it K a u k a s o s,—this being another Kaukasos and distinct from the Skythian, so that the story went that Alexander penetrated to the regions beyond Kaukasos.

---

be a corrupted form of "Indicus Caucasus," the name given to the range by the Makedonians, either to flatter Alexander, or because they regarded it as a continuation of Kaukasos. Arrian, however, and others held it to be a continuation of T a u r o s. The mountains belonging to the range which lie to the north of the Kâbul river are called N i s h a d h a, (see Lassen, *Ind. Alt.* I. p. 22, note), a Sanskṛit word which appears perhaps in the form Paropanisos, which is that given by Ptolemy. According to Pliny, the Skythians called Mount Caucasus G r a u c a s i s, a word which represents the Indian name of Paropamisos, G r a v a k s h a s, which Ritter translates "*splendentes rupium montes.*" According to General Cunningham, the Mount P a r e s h or A p a r a s i n of the *Zendavesta* corresponds with the Paropamisos of the Greeks. *Paro*, the first part of the word, St.-Martin says, represents undoubtedly the P a r u or P a r u t a of the local dialects (in Zend, *Purouta* meaning *mountain*). He acknowledges, however, that he cannot assign any reason why the syllable *pa* has been intercalated between the vocables *paru* and *nishada* to form the P a r o p a n i s a d æ of the Greek. The first Greek writer who mentions the range is Aristotle, who calls it Parnassos: see his *Meteorol.* I. 18. H i n d û K u s h generally designates now the eastern part of the range, and P a r o p a m i s o s the western. According to Sir Alexander Burnes, the name Hindû Kush is unknown to the Afghâns, but there is a particular peak and also a pass bearing that name between Afghânistân and Turkestân.—E m o d o s (other forms—Emoda, Emodon, Hemodes). The name generally designated that part of the Himâlayan range which extended along Nepâl and Bhûtan and onward towards the ocean. Lassen derives the word from the Sanskṛit *haimavata*, in Prâkṛit *haimota*, 'snowy.' If this be so, 'Hemodos' is the more correct form. Another derivation refers the word to "*hêmâdri*" (*hema*, gold, and *adri*, mountain), 'the golden mountains,' —so called either because they were thought to contain gold mines, or because of the aspect they presented when their snowy peaks reflected the golden effulgence of sunset.

On the west the boundaries of India are marked by the river Indus all the way to the great ocean into which it pours its waters, which it does by two mouths. These mouths are not close to each other, like the five mouths of the Ister (Danube), but diverge like those of the Nile, by which the Egyptian delta is formed. The Indus in like manner makes an Indian delta, which is not inferior in area to the Egyptian, and is called in the Indian tongue Pattala.¶

On the south-west, again, and on the south, India is bounded by the great ocean just mentioned, which also forms its boundary on the east. The parts toward the south about Pattala and the river Indus were seen by Alexander and many of the Greeks, but in an eastern direction Alex-

¶ Pattala.—The name of the Delta was properly Pâṭalene, and Pâṭala was its capital. This was situated at the head of the Delta, where the western stream of the Indus bifurcated. Ṭhaṭha has generally been regarded as its modern representative, but General Cunningham would "almost certainly" identify it with Nirankol or Haidarâbâd, of which Pâṭalpur and Pâṭaśila ('flat rock') were old appellations. With regard to the name Pâṭala he suggests that "it may have been derived from *Pâṭala*, the trumpet flower" (*Bignonia suaveolens*), "in allusion to the trumpet shape of the province included between the eastern and western branches of the mouth of the Indus, as the two branches as they approach the sea curve outward like the mouth of a trumpet." Ritter, however, says:—"Pâtâla is the designation bestowed by the Brâhmaṇs on all the provinces in the west towards sunset, in antithesis to Prasiaka (the eastern realm) in Ganges-land: for *Pâṭâla* is the mythological name in Sanskṛit of the under-world, and consequently of the land of the west." Arrian's estimate of the magnitude of the Delta is somewhat excessive. The length of its base, from the Pitti to the Kori mouth, was less than 1000 stadia, while that of the Egyptian Delta was 1300.

ander did not penetrate beyond the river H y p h a s i s, though a few authors have described the country as far as the river G a n g e s and the parts near its mouths and the city of P a l i m b o t h r a, which is the greatest in India, and situated near the Ganges.

III. *I shall now state the dimensions of India*, and in doing so let me follow E r a t o s t h e n ê s of Kyrenê as the safest authority, for this Eratosthenês made its circuit a subject of special inquiry.* He states, then, that if a line be drawn from Mount Tauros, where the Indus has its springs, along the course of that river and as far as the great ocean and the mouths of the Indus, this side of India will measure 13,000 stadia.† But the contrary side, which diverges from the same point of Tauros and runs along the Eastern Sea, he makes of a much different length, for there is a headland which projects far out into the

---

* Schmieder, from whose text I translate, has here altered (perhaps unnecessarily) the reading of the MSS. from τῆς περιόδου to γῆς περιόδου. The measurements given by Strabo are more accurate than those of Arrian. They are, however, not at all wide of the mark; General Cunningham, indeed, remarks that their close agreement with the actual size of the country is very remarkable, and shows, he adds, that the Indians, even at that early date in their history, had a very accurate knowledge of the form and extent of their native land.

† The Olympic stadium, which was in general use throughout Greece, contained 600 Greek feet = 625 Roman feet. or 606¾ English feet. The Roman mile contained eight stadia, being about half a stadium less than an English mile. The *schoinos* (mentioned below) was = 2 Persian parasangs = 60 stadia, but was generally taken at half that length.

sea, and this headland is in length about 3,000 stadia. The eastern side of India would thus by his calculation measure 16,000 stadia, and this is what he assigns as the breadth of India. The length, again, from west to east as far as the city of Palimbothra he sets down, he says, as it had been measured by *schœni*, since there existed a royal highway, and he gives it as 10,000 stadia. But as for the parts beyond they were not measured with equal accuracy. Those, however, who write from mere hearsay allege that the breadth of India, inclusive of the headland which projects into the sea, is about 10,000 stadia, while the length measured from the coast is about 20,000 stadia. But Ktêsias of Knidos says that India equals in size all the rest of Asia, which is absurd; while Onesikritós as absurdly declares that it is the third part of the whole earth. Nearchos, again, says that it takes a journey of four months to traverse even the plain of India; while Megasthenês, who calls the breadth of India its extent from east to west, though others call this its length, says that where shortest the breadth is 16,000 stadia, and that its length—by which he means its extent from north to south—is, where narrowest, 22,300 stadia. But, whatever be its dimensions, the rivers of India are certainly the largest to be found in all Asia. The mightiest are the Ganges and the Indus, from which the country receives its name. Both are greater than the Egyptian Nile and the Skythian Ister even if their streams were united into one. I think, too, that even the Akesinês is greater than either the Ister or the Nile where it joins the Indus after receiving its tributaries the Hydaspês and the Hydraôtês, since it is at that point so much as 300 stadia in breadth. It is also possible that there are even many other larger rivers which take their course through India.

IV. But I am unable to give with assurance of being accurate any information regarding the regions beyond the Hyphasis, since the progress of Alexander was arrested by that river. But to recur to the two greatest rivers, the Ganges and the Indus. Megasthenês states that of the two the Ganges is much the larger, and other writers who mention the Ganges agree with him; for, besides being of ample volume even where it issues from its springs, it receives as tributaries the river Kaïnas, and the Erannoboas, and the Kossoanos, which are all navigable. It receives, besides, the river Sonos and the Sittokatis, and the Solomatis, which are also navigable, and also the Kondochatês, and the Sambos, and the Magôn, and the Agoranis, and the Omalis. Moreover there fall into it the Kommenasês, a great river, and the Kakouthis, and the Andomatis, which flows from the dominions of the Madyandinoi, an Indian tribe. In addition to all these, the **A m y s t i s**, which flows past the city **K a t a d u p a**, and the **O x y m a g i s** from the dominions of a tribe called the **P a z a l a i**, and the **E r r e n y s i s** from the **M a t h a i**, an Indian tribe, unite with the Ganges.‡

---

‡ Arrian here enumerates seventeen tributaries of the Ganges. The number is given as nineteen by Pliny, who adds the Prinas and the Jomanês, which Arrian elsewhere (cap. viii.) mentions under the name of the Jobares. These tributaries have been nearly all identified by the researches of such learned men as Rennel, Wilford, Schlegel, Lassen, and Schwanbeck. M. de St.-Martin, in reviewing their conclusions, clears up a few points which they had left in doubt, or wherein he thinks they had erred. I shall now show how each of the nineteen tributaries has been identified.

K a ï n a s.—This has been identified with the Kan, or Kane, or Kêna, which, however, is only indirectly a tributary of the Ganges, as it falls into the Jamnâ. The Sanskṛit name of the Kan is Śena, and Schwanbeck (p. 36) objects to the identification that the Greeks invariably represent the Sanskṛit ê by their η, and never by $\alpha\iota$. St.-Martin attaches no importance to this objection, and gives the Sanskṛit equivalent as Kâiana.

E r r a n o b o a s.—As Arrian informs us (cap. x.) that P a l i m b o t h r a (P â ṭ a l i p u t r a, Pâṭnâ) was situated at the confluence of this river with the Ganges, it must be identified with the river S ô n, which formerly joined the Ganges a little above Bankipur, the western suburb of Pâṭnâ, from which its embouchure is now 16 miles distant and higher up the Ganges. The word no doubt represents the Sanskṛit H i r a n y a v â h a ('carrying gold') or Hiranyabâhu ('having golden arms'), which are both poetical names of the Sôn. Megasthenês, however, and Arrian, both make the Erannoboas and the Sôn to be distinct rivers, and hence some would identify the former with the G a n d a k (Sanskṛit G a n d a k i), which, according to Lassen, was called by the Buddhists H i r a n y a v a t i, or 'the golden.' It is, however, too small a stream to suit the description of the Erannoboas, that it was the largest river in India after the Ganges and Indus. The Sôn may perhaps in the time of Megasthenês have joined the Ganges by two channels, which he may have mistaken for separate rivers.

Regarding these streams Megasthenês asserts that none of them is inferior to the Mai-

---

Kosoanos.—Cosoagus is the form of the name in Pliny, and hence it has been taken to be the representative of the Sanskṛit Kaushiki, the river now called the Kosi. Schwanbeck, however, thinks it represents the Sanskṛit *Kośâvâha* ('treasure-bearing'), and that it is therefore an epithet of the Sôn, like Hiranyavâha, which has the same meaning. It seems somewhat to favour this view that Arrian in his enumeration places the Kosoanos between the Erannoboas and the Sôn.

Sônos.—The Sôn, which now joins the Ganges ten miles above Dinâpur. The word is considered to be a contraction of the Sanskṛit Suvarṇa (Suvanna), 'golden,' and may have been given as a name to the river either because its sands were yellow, or because they contained gold dust.

Sittokatis.—It has not been ascertained what river was denoted by this name, but St.-Martin thinks it may be the representative of the Sadâkântâ—a river now unknown, but mentioned in the *Mahâbhârata* along with the Kouśadhârâ (the Kosi), the Sadânîrâ (the Karatoyâ), and the Adhrichya (the Atreyi), from which it is evident that it belonged to the northern parts of Bengal.

Solomatis.—It has not been ascertained what river was denoted by this name. General Cunningham in one of his maps gives the Solomatis as a name of the Saranju or Sarju, a tributary of the Ghagrâ; while Benfey and others would identify it with the famous Sarasvatî or Sarsuti, which, according to the legends, after disappearing underground, joined the Ganges at Allahâbâd. There is more probability, however, in Lassen's suggestion, that the word somewhat erroneously transliterates *Śarâvatî*, the name of a city of Kôśala mentioned by Kâlidâsa and in the Purâṇas, where it appears generally in the form *Śravastî*. This city stood on a river which, though nowhere mentioned by name, must also have been called *Śarâvatî*, since there is an obvious connexion between that name and the name by which the river of that district is now known—the Rapti.

Kondochates.—Now the Gandak,—in Sanskṛit, Gandaki or Gandakavati (ῥινοκερόεις),—because of its abounding in a kind of alligator having a horn-like projection on its nose. It skirted the eastern border of Kôśala, joining the Ganges opposite Palibothra,

Sambos.—This has no Sanskṛit equivalent. It perhaps designated the Gumṭî, which is said to go by the name of the Sambou at a part of its course below Lucknow.

a n d r o s, even at the navigable part of its course; and as for the **G a n g e s**, it has a breadth where

---

M a g o n.—According to Mannert the R â m g a ṅ g â, but much more probably the Mahânada, now the M a h o n a, the principal river of Magadha, which joins the Ganges not far below Pâṭnâ.

A g o r a n i s.—According to Rennel the G h a g r â—a word derived from the Sanskṛit G h a r g h a r a ('of gurgling sound'), but according to St.-Martin it must be some one or other of the G a o u r î s so abundant in the river nomenclature of Northern India. The vulgar form is G a u r a n a.

O m a l i s has not been identified, but Schwanbeck remarks that the word closely agrees with the Sanskṛit V i m a l a ('stainless'), a common epithet of rivers.

K o m m e n a s e s.—Rennel and Lassen identify this with the K a r m a ṇ â s a (*bonorum operum destructrix*), a small river which joins the Ganges above Baxâr. According to a Hindu legend, whoever touches the water of this river loses all the merit of his good works, this being transferred to the nymph of the stream.

K a k o u t h i s.—Mannert erroneously takes this to be the G u m t î. Lassen identifies it with the Kakouttha of the Buddhist chronicles, and hence with the Bagmatti, the Bhagavati of Sanskṛit.

A n d ô m a t i s.—Thought by Lassen to be connected with the Sanskṛit Andhamati (*tenebricosus*), which he would identify, therefore, with the T â m a s â, (now the Tonsa), the two names being identical in meaning; but, as the river came from the country of the M a d y a n d i n i (Sanskṛit M a d h y a n d i n a, *meridionalis*),—that is, *the people of the South*,—Wilford's conjecture that the Andomatis is the Dammuda, the river which flows by Bardwân, is more likely to be correct. The Sanskṛit name of the Dammuda is Dharmadaya.

A m y s t i s.—The city Katadupa, which this river passes, Wilford would identify with Katwa or Cutwa, in Lower Bengal, which is situated on the western branch of the delta of the Ganges at the confluence of the Adji. As the Sanskṛit form of the name of Katva should be Katadvîpa '(*dvîpa*, an island'), M. de St.-Martin thinks this conjecture has much probability in its favour. The Amystis may therefore be the A d j î, or A j a v a t i as it is called in Sanskṛit.

O x y m a g i s.—The Pazalai or Passalai, called in Sanskṛit P a n k a l a, inhabited the Doâb, and through this or the region adjacent flowed the Ikshumati ('abounding in sugarcane'). O x y m a g i s very probably represented this

narrowest of one hundred stadia, while in many places it spreads out into lakes, so that when the country happens to be flat and destitute of elevations the opposite shores cannot be seen from each other. The Indus presents also, he says, similar characteristics. The Hydraôtês, flowing from the dominions of the Kambistholi, falls into the Akesinês after receiving the Hyphasis in its passage through the Astrybai, as well as the Saranges from the Kekians, and the Neudros from the Attakenoi. The Hydaspês again, rising in the dominions of the Oxydrakai, and bringing with it the Sinaros, received in the dominion of the Arispai, falls itself into the Akesinês, while the Akesinês joins the Indus in the dominions of the Malloi, but not until it has received the waters of a great

---

name, since the letters Γ and T in Greek could readily be confounded. The form of the name in Megasthenês may have been Oxymetis.

Errenysis closely corresponds to Vârânasi, the name of Banâras in Sanskṛit,—so called from the rivers Vârâna and Asi, which join the Ganges in its neighbourhood. The Mathai, it has been thought, may be the people of Magadha. St.-Martin would fix their position in the time of Megasthenês in the country between the lower part of the Gumṭî and the Ganges, adding that as the *Journal* of Hiwen Thsâng places their capital, Mâtipura, at a little distance to the east of the upper Ganges near Gaṅgâdvâra, now Hardwâr, they must have extended their name and dominion by the traveller's time far beyond their original bounds. The Prinas, which Arrian has omitted, St.-Martin would identify with the Tâmasâ, which is otherwise called the Parnâsâ, and belongs to the same part of the country as the Kaïnas, in connexion with which Pliny mentions the Prinas.

tributary, the Toutapos. Augmented by all these confluents the Akesinês succeeds in imposing its name on the combined waters, and still retains it till it unites with the Indus. The Kôphen, too, falls into the Indus, rising in Peukelaïtis, and bringing with it the Malantos, and the Soastos, and the Garroia. Higher up than these, the Parenos and Saparnos, at no great distance from each other, empty themselves into the Indus, as does also the Soanos, which comes without a tributary from the hill-country of the Abissareans.§

---

§ *Tributaries of the Indus* :—Arrian has here named only 13 tributaries of the Indus (in Sanskṛit Sindhu, in the *Periplûs of the Erythræan Sea* Sinthos), but in his *Anabasis* (v. 6) he states that the number was 15, which is also the number given by Strabo. Pliny reckons them at 19.

Hydraôtês.—Other forms are Rhouadis and Hyarotis. It is now called the Râvi, the name being a contraction of the Sanskṛit Airâvati, which means 'abounding in water,' or 'the daughter of Airâvat,' the elephant of Indra, who is said to have generated the river by striking his tusk against the rock whence it issues. His name has reference to his 'ocean' origin. The name of the Kambistholai does not occur elsewhere. Schwanbeck (p. 33) conjectures that it may represent the Sanskṛit Kapisthala, 'ape-land,' the letter *m* being inserted, as in 'Palimbothra.' He rejects Wilson's suggestion that the people may be identical with the Kambojæ. Arrian errs in making the Hyphasis a tributary of the Hydraôtês, for it falls into the Akesinês below its junction with that river. See on this point St.-Martin, *E'tude*, p. 396.

Hyphasis (other forms are Bibasis, Hypasis, and Hypanis).—In Sanskṛit the Vipâśa, and now the Byasa or Bias. It lost its name on being joined by the Śatadru, 'the hundred-channelled,' the Zaradros of Ptolemy, now the Satlej. The Astrobai are not mentioned by any writer except Arrian.

Saranges.—According to Schwanbeck, this word represents the Sanskrit Saranga, 'six-limbed.' It is not known what river it designated. The Kekians, through

According to Megasthenês most of these rivers are navigable. We ought not, therefore, to

---

whose country it flowed, were called in Sanskṛit, according to Lassen, Sekaya.

Neudros is not known. The Attakenoi are likewise unknown, unless their name is another form of *Assakenoi*.

Hydaspês.—Bidaspês is the form in Ptolemy, which makes a nearer approach to its Sanskṛit name—the Vitasta. It is now the Behut or Jhelam; called also by the inhabitants on its banks tho Bedusta, 'widely spread.' It is the "fabulosus Hydaspes" of Horace, and the "Medus (*i.e.* Eastern) Hydaspes" of Virgil. It formed the western boundary of the dominions of Pôros.

Akesinês.—Now the Chenâb: its Sanskṛit name *Asikni* ('dark-coloured') is met with in the hymns of the Vêda. It was called afterwards Chandrabhâga (*portio lunæ*). This would be represented in Greek by Sandrophagos,—a word in sound so like *Androphagos* or *Ale-xandrophagos* ('devourer of Alexander') that the followers of the great conqueror changed the name to avoid the evil omen,—the more so, perhaps, on account of the disaster which befell the Makedonian fleet at the turbulent junction of the river with the Hydaspês. Ptolemy gives its name as *Sandabaga* (*Sandabala* by an error on the part of copyists), which is an exact transcription of the Prâkṛit *Chandabaga*, of which word the *Cantabra* of Pliny is a greatly altered form. The Malli, in whose country this river joins the Indus, are the Malava of Sanskṛit, whose name is prescribed in the *Multân* of the present day.

Toutapos.—Probably the lower part of the Śatadru or Satlej.

Kôphên.—Another form of the name, used by Strabo, Pliny, &c., is Kophês, -êtis. It is now the Kâbul river. The three rivers here named as its tributaries probably correspond to the Suvâstu, Gaurî, and Kampana mentioned in the 6th book of the *Mahâbhârata*. The Soastos is no doubt the Suvastu, and the Garœa the Gaurî. Curtius and Strabo call the Suastus the Choaspes. According to Mannert the Suastus and the Garœa or Guræus were identical. Lassen, however (*Ind. Alterthums*. 2nd ed. II. 673 ff.), would identify the Suastus with the modern Suwad or Svât, and the Garæus with its tributary the Panjkora; and this is the view adopted by Cunningham. The Malamantos some would identify with the Choes (mentioned by Arrian, *Anabasis* iv. 25), which is probably represented by the Kameh or Khonar, the largest of the tributaries of the

distrust what we are told regarding the Indus and the Ganges, that they are beyond comparison greater than the Ister and the Nile. In the case of the Nile we know that it does not receive any tributary, but that, on the contrary, in its passage through Egypt its waters are drawn off to fill the canals. As for the Ister, it is but an insignificant stream at its sources, and though it no doubt receives many confluents, still these are neither equal in number to the confluents of the Indus and

---

Kâbul; others, however, with the Panjkora, while Cunningham takes it to be the Bâra, a tributary which joins the Kâbul from the south. With regard to the name Kophes this author remarks:—"The name of Kophes is as old as the time of the *Vedas*, in which the Kubhâ river is mentioned [Roth first pointed this out;—conf. Lassen, *ut sup.*] as an affluent of the Indus; and, as it is not an Âryan word, I infer that the name must have been applied to the Kâbul river before the Âryan occupation, or at least as early as B.C. 2500. In the classical writers we find the Choes, Kophes, and Choaspes rivers to the west of the Indus; and at the present day we have the Kunar, the Kuram, and the Gomal rivers to the west, and the Kunihar river to the east of the Indus,—all of which are derived from the Skythian *ku*, 'water.' It is the guttural form of the Assyrian *hu* in 'Euphrates' and 'Eulæus,' and of the Turki *su* and Tibetan *chu*, all of which mean 'water' or 'river.' Ptolemy the Geographer mentions a city called Kabura, situated on the banks of the Kophen, and a people called Kabolitæ.

Parenos.—Probably the modern Burindu.

Saparnos.—Probably the Abbasin.

Soanus represents the Sanskṛit Suvana, 'the sun,' or 'fire'—now the Svan. The Abissaræans, from whose country it comes, may be the Abisara of Sanskṛit: Lassen, *Ind. Alt.* II. 163. A king called Abisarês is mentioned by Arrian in his *Anabasis* (iv. 7). It may be here remarked that the names of the Indian kings, as given by the Greek writers, were in general the names slightly modified of the people over whom they ruled.

Ganges, nor are they navigable like them, if we except a very few,—as, for instance, the Inn, and Save which I have myself seen. The Inn joins the Ister where the Noricans march with the Rhætians, and the Save in the dominions of the Pannonians, at a place which is called Taurunum.|| Some one may perhaps know other navigable tributaries of the Danube, but the number certainly cannot be great.

V. Now if anyone wishes to state a reason to account for the number and magnitude of the Indian rivers let him state it. As for myself I have written on this point, as on others, from hearsay; for Megasthenês has given the names even of other rivers which beyond both the Ganges and the Indus pour their waters into the Eastern Ocean and the outer basin of the Southern Ocean, so that he asserts that there are eight-and-fifty Indian rivers which are all of them navigable. But even Megasthenês, so far as appears, did not travel over much of India, though no doubt he saw more of it than those who came with Alexander the son of Philip, for, as he tells us, he resided at the court of Sandrakottos, the greatest king in India, and also at the court of Pôros, who was still greater than he. This same Megasthenês then informs us that the Indians neither invade other men, nor do other men invade the

|| Taurunum.—The modern Semlin.

Indians: for S e s o s t r i s the Egyptian, after having overrun the greater part of Asia, and advanced with his army as far as Europe, returned home; and I d a n t h y r s o s the Skythian issuing from Skythia, subdued many nations of Asia, and carried his victorious arms even to the borders of Egypt; and S e m i r a m i s, again, the Assyrian queen, took in hand an expedition against India, but died before she could execute her design: and thus Alexander was the only conqueror who actually invaded the country. And regarding D i o n y s o s many traditions are current to the effect that he also made an expedition into India, and subjugated the Indians before the days of Alexander. But of H e r a k l ê s tradition does not say much. Of the expedition, however, which Bakkhos led, the city of N y s a is no mean monument, while Mount M ê r o s is yet another, and the ivy which grows thereon, and the practice observed by the Indians themselves of marching to battle with drums and cymbals, and of wearing a spotted dress such as was worn by the Bacchanals of Dionysos. On the other hand, there are but few memorials of Heraklês, and it may be doubted whether even these are genuine: for the assertion that Heraklês was not able to take the rock A o r n o s, which Alexander seized by force of arms, seems to me all a Makedonian vaunt, quite of a piece with their calling P a r a p a m i s o s—K a u k a s o s, though it had no connexion at all with K a u k asos. In the same spirit, when they noticed a cave in the dominions of the Parapamisadai, they asserted that it was the cave of Prometheus the Titan, in which he had been suspended for stealing the fire.¶ So also when they came among the Sibai, an Indian tribe, and noticed that they wore skins, they declared that the Sibai were descended from those who belonged to the expedition of Heraklês and had been left behind: for, besides being dressed in skins, the Sibai carry a cudgel, and brand on the backs of their oxen the representation of a club, wherein the Makedonians recognized a memorial of the club of Heraklês. But if any one believes all this, then this must be another Heraklês,—not the Theban, but either the Tyrian or the Egyptian, or even some great king who belonged to the upper country which lies not far from India.

VI. Let this be *said by way of* a digression to discredit the accounts which some writers have given of the Indians beyond the Hyphasis, for those writers who were in Alexander's expedition are not altogether unworthy of our faith when they describe India as far as the Hyphasis. *Beyond that limit we have no real knowledge of the country:* since this is the sort of account which Megasthenês gives us of an Indian river:—Its name is the Silas; it flows from a fountain,

---

¶ The Cave of Prometheus.—Probably one of the vast caves in the neighbourhood of Bamian.

called after the river, through the dominions of the S i l æ a n s, who again are called after the river and the fountain; the water of the river manifests this singular property—that there is nothing which it can buoy up, nor anything which can swim or float in it, but everything sinks down to the bottom, so that there is nothing in the world so thin and unsubstantial as this water.* But *to proceed.* Rain falls in India during the summer, especially on the mountains P a r a p a- m i s o s and E m o d o s and the range of I m a o s, and the rivers which issue from these are large and muddy. Rain during the same season falls also on the plains of India, so that much of the country is submerged: and indeed the army of Alexander was obliged at the time of midsummer to retreat in haste from the A k e s i n ê s, because its waters overflowed the adjacent plains. So we may by analogy infer from these facts that as the N i l e is subject to similar inundations, it is probable that rain falls during the summer on the mountains of Ethiopia, and that the Nile swollen with these rains overflows its banks and inundates Egypt. We find, at any rate, that this river, like those we have mentioned, flows at the same season of the year with a muddy current, which could not be the case if it flowed from melting snows, nor yet if its waters were driven back from its

---

* See note, p. 65.

mouth by the force of the Etesian winds which blow throughout the hot season,† and that it should flow from melting snow is all the more unlikely as snow cannot fall upon the Ethiopian mountains, on account of the burning heat; but that rain should fall on them, as on the Indian mountains, is not beyond probability, since India in other respects besides is not unlike Ethiopia. Thus the Indian rivers, like the Nile in Ethiopia and Egypt, breed crocodiles, while some of them have fish and monstrous creatures such as are found in the Nile, with the exception only of the hippopotamus, though Onesikritos asserts that they breed this animal also. With regard to the inhabitants, there is no great difference in type of figure between the Indians and the Ethiopians, though the Indians, no doubt, who live in the south-west bear a somewhat closer resemblance to the Ethiopians, being of black complexion and black-haired, though they are not so snub-nosed nor have the hair so curly; while the Indians who live further to the north are in person liker the Egyptians.

VII. The Indian tribes, Megasthenês tells us, number in all 118. [And I so far agree with him as to allow that they must be indeed numerous, but when he gives such a precise estimate I am at a loss to conjecture how he

† Cf. Herodotus, II. 20-27.

arrived at it, for the greater part of India he did not visit, nor is mutual intercourse maintained between all the tribes.] He tells us further that the Indians were in old times nomadic, like those Skythians who did not till the soil, but roamed about in their wagons, as the seasons varied, from one part of Skythia to another, neither dwelling in towns nor worshipping in temples; and that the Indians likewise had neither towns nor temples of the gods, but were so barbarous that they wore the skins of such wild animals as they could kill, and subsisted on the bark of trees; that these trees were called in Indian speech *tala*, and that there grew on them, as there grows at the tops of the palm-trees, a fruit resembling balls of wool;‡ that they subsisted also on such wild animals as they could catch, eating the flesh raw,—before, at least, the coming of Dionysos into India. Dionysos, however, when he came and had conquered the people, founded cities and gave laws to these cities, and introduced the use of wine among the Indians, as he had done among the Greeks, and taught them to sow the land, himself supplying seeds for the purpose,—either because Triptọlemos, when he was sent by Dêmêter to sow all the earth, did not reach these parts, or this must have been some Dionysos who came to India before Triptolemos, and gave the people the seeds of

‡ Tala.—The fan-palm, the *Borassus flabelliformis* of botany.

cultivated plants. It is also said that Dionysos first yoked oxen to the plough, and made many of the Indians husbandmen instead of nomads, and furnished them with the implements of agriculture; and that the Indians worship the other gods, and Dionysos himself in particular, with cymbals and drums, because he so taught them; and that he also taught them the Satyric dance, or, as the Greeks call it, the *Kordax*; and that he instructed the Indians to let their hair grow long in honour of the god, and to wear the turban; and that he taught them to anoint themselves with unguents, so that even up to the time of Alexander the Indians were marshalled for battle to the sound of cymbals and drums.

VIII. But when he was leaving India, after having established the new order of things, he appointed, it is said, Spatembas, one of his companions and the most conversant with Bakkhic matters, to be the king of the country. When Spatembas died his son Boudyas succeeded to the sovereignty; the father reigning over the Indians fifty-two years, and the son twenty; the son of the latter, whose name was Kradeuas, duly inherited the kingdom, and thereafter the succession was generally hereditary, but that when a failure of heirs occurred in the royal house the Indians elected their sovereigns on the principle of merit; Hêrakles, however, who is currently reported to have come *as a stranger* into the country, is said to have been in reality a native of India. This Hêrakles is held in especial honour by the S o u r a s e n o i, an Indian tribe who possess two large cities, M e t h o r a and C l e i s o b o r a, and through whose country flows a navigable river called the I o b a r e s. But the dress which this Hêrakles wore, Megasthenês tells us, resembled that of the T h e b a n H ê r a k l e s, as the Indians themselves admit. It is further said that he had a very numerous progeny of male children born to him in India (for, like his Theban namesake, he married many wives), but that he had only one daughter. The name of this child was P a n d a i a, and the land in which she was born, and with the sovereignty of which Hêrakles entrusted her, was called after her name, P a n d a i a, and she received from the hands of her father 500 elephants, a force of cavalry 4000 strong, and another of infantry consisting of about 130,000 men. Some Indian writers say further of Hêrakles that when he was going over the world and ridding land and sea of whatever evil monsters infested them, he found in the sea an ornament for women, which even to this day the Indian traders who bring us their wares eagerly buy up and carry away to foreign markets, while it is even more eagerly bought up by the wealthy Romans of to-day, as it was wont to be by the wealthy Greeks long ago. This article is the sea-pearl, called in the Indian tongue *margarita*. But Hêrakles, it is said, appreciating its beauty as a wearing ornament, caused it to be brought from all the sea into India, that he might adorn with it the person of his daughter.

Megasthenês informs us that the oyster which yields this pearl is there fished for with nets, and that in these same parts the oysters live in the sea in shoals like bee-swarms: for oysters, like bees, have a king or a queen, and if any one is lucky enough to catch the king he readily encloses in the net all the rest of the shoal, but if the king makes his escape there is no chance that the others can be caught. The fishermen allow the fleshy parts of such as they catch to rot away, and keep the bone, which forms the ornament: for the pearl in India is worth thrice its weight in refined gold, gold being a product of the Indian mines.

IX. Now in that part of the country where the daughter of Hêrakles reigned as queen, it is said that the women when seven years old are of marriageable age, and that the men live at most forty years, and that on this subject there is a tradition current among the Indians to the effect that Hêrakles, whose daughter was born to him late in life, when he saw that his end was near, and he knew no man his equal in rank to whom he could give her in marriage, had incestuous intercourse with the girl when she was seven years of age, in order that a race of kings sprung from their common blood might be left to rule over India; that Hêrakles therefore made her of suitable age for marriage, and that in consequence the whole nation over which Pandaia reigned obtained this same privilege from her father. Now to me it seems that, even if Hêrakles could have done a thing so marvellous, he could also have made himself longer-lived, in order to have intercourse with his daughter when she was of mature age. But in fact, if the age at which the women there are marriageable is correctly stated, this is quite consistent, it seems to me, with what is said of the men's age,—that those who live longest die at forty; for men who come so much sooner to old age, and with old age to death, must of course flower into full manhood as much earlier as their life ends earlier. It follows hence that men of thirty would there be in their green old age, and young men would at twenty be past puberty, while the stage of of full puberty would be reached about fifteen. And, quite compatibly with this, the women might be marriageable at the age of seven. And why not, when Megasthenês declares that the very fruits of the country ripen faster than fruits elsewhere, and decay faster?

From the time of Dionysos to Sandrakottos the Indians counted 153 kings and a period of 6042 years, but among these a republic was thrice established * * * * and another to 300 years, and another to 120 years.§ The

§ It is not known from what sources Megasthenês derived these figures, which are extremely modest when compared with those of Indian chronology, where, as in geology, years are hardly reckoned but in myriads. For a notice of

Indians also tell us that Dionysos was earlier than Hêrakles by fifteen generations, and that except him no one made a hostile invasion of India,—not even Kyros the son of Kambysês, although he undertook an expedition against the Skythians, and otherwise showed himself the most enterprising monarch in all Asia; but that Alexander indeed came and overthrew in war all whom he attacked, and would even have conquered the whole world had his army been willing *to follow him*. On the other hand, a sense of justice, they say, prevented any Indian king from attempting conquest beyond the limits of India.

X. It is further said that the Indians do not rear monuments to the dead, but consider the virtues which men have displayed in life, and the songs in which their praises are celebrated, sufficient to preserve their memory after death. But of their cities it is said that the number is so great that it cannot be stated with precision, but that such cities as are situated on the banks of rivers or on the sea-coast are built of wood, for were they built of brick they would not last long —so destructive are the rains, and also the rivers when they overflow their banks and inundate the plains; those cities, however, which stand on commanding situations and lofty eminences are built of brick and mud. The greatest city in India is

---

the Magadha dynasties see Elphinstone's *History of India*, bk. III. cap. iii.

that which is called Palimbothra, in the dominions of the Prasians,|| where the streams of the Erannoboas and the Ganges unite,—the Ganges being the greatest of all rivers, and the Erannoboas being perhaps the third largest of Indian rivers, though greater than the greatest rivers elsewhere; but it is smaller than the Ganges where it falls into it. Megasthenês says further of this city that the inhabited part of it stretched on either side to an extreme length of eighty stadia, and that its breadth was fifteen stadia, and that a ditch encompassed it all round, which was six *plethra* in breadth and thirty cubits in depth, and that the wall was crowned with five hundred and seventy towers and had four-and-sixty gates.¶ The same writer tells us further this

---

|| The Prasioi.—In the notes which the reader will find at pp. 9 and 57, the accepted explanation of the name *Prasioi*, by which the Greeks designated the people of Magadha, has been stated. General Cunningham explains it differently:—"Strabo and Pliny," he says, "agree with Arrian in calling the people of Palibothra by the name of Prasii, which modern writers have unanimously referred to the Sanskrit Prâchya, or 'eastern.' But it seems to me that Prasii is only the Greek form of Palâsa or Parâsa, which is an actual and well-known name of Magadha, of which Palibothra was the capital. It obtained this name from the *Palâsa*, or *Butea frondosa*, which still grows as luxuriantly in the province as in the time of Hiwen Thsâng. The common form of the name is Parâs, or when quickly pronounced Prâs, which I take to be the true original of the Greek Prasii. This derivation is supported by the spelling of the name given by Curtius, who calls the people Pharrasii, which is an almost exact transcript of the Indian name Parâsiya. The Praxiakos of Ælian is only the derivative from Palâsaka."

¶ The more usual and the more accurate form of the name is *Palibothra*, a transcription of *Pâliputra*, the spoken

remarkable fact about India, that all the Indians are free, and not one of them is a slave. The

---

form of *Pâṭaliputra*, the name of the ancient capital of Magadha, and a name still occasionally applied to the city of Pâṭnâ, which is its modern representative. The word, which means *the son of the trumpet-flower* (*Bignonia suaveolens*), appears in several different forms. A provincial form, *Pâṭaliputrika*, is common in the popular tales. The form in tbe *Panchatantra* is Pâṭaliputra, which Wilson (Introd. to the *Dasa Kamara Charitra*) considered to be the true original name of the city of which Pâṭaliputra was a mere corruption,—sanctioned, however, by common usage. In a Sanskṛit treatise of geography of a somewhat recent date, called the *Kshetra Samasa*, the form of the name is *Pâlibhâtta*, which is a near approach to *Palibotra*. The Ceylon chroniclers invariably wrote the name as Pâtiliputto, and in the inscription of Aśôka at Girnâr it is written Pâṭaliputta. The earliest name of the place, according to the *Râmâyaṇa*, was Kauśambi, as having been founded by Kuśa, the father of the famous sage Viśvamitra. It was also called, especially by the poets, *Pashpapura* or *Kusumapura*, which has the same meaning—'*the city of flowers*.' This city, though the least ancient of all the greater capitals in Gangetic India, was destined to become the most famous of them all. The *Vayu Purâna* attributes its foundation to Udaya (called also Udayaśva), who mounted the throne of Magadha in the year 519 B.C., or 24 years after the *Nirvâna* (*Vishnu Purâna*, p. 467, n. 15; Lassen, *Ind. Alt.* II. p. 63). Pâṭaliputra did not, however, according to the Cingalese chronicles, become the residence of the kings of Magadha till the reign of Kâlâśôka, who ascended the throne 453 B. C. Under Chandragupta (the Sandrakottos of the Greeks), who founded the Buddhistic dynasty of the Mauriyas, the kingdom was extended from the mouths of the Ganges to the regions beyond the Indus, and became in fact the paramount power in India. Nor was Pâṭaliputra—to judge from the account of its size and splendour given here by Arrian, and in Frag. XXV. by Strabo, who both copied it from Megasthenês—unworthy to be the capital of so great an empire. Its happy position at the confluence of the Sôn and Ganges, and opposite the junction of the Gandak with their united stream, naturally made it a great centre of commerce, which would no doubt greatly increase its wealth and prosperity. Aśôka, who was third in succession from Chandragupta, and who made Buddhism the state religion, in his inscription on the rock at Dhâuli in Katak, gives it the title of *Metropolis of the Religion*, *i.e.* of Buddhism. The wooden wall by which, as Megasthenês tells us, it was surrounded, was still standing

Lakedaimonians and the Indians here so far agree. The Lakedaimonians, however, hold

---

seven centuries later than his time, for it was seen about the beginning of the 5th century after Christ by the Chinese traveller Fa-Hian, who thus writes of Pâliputra, which he calls Pa-lian-fu :—"The city was the capital of king A-you (Aśôka). The palaces of the king which are in the city have walls of which the stones have been collected by the genii. The carvings and the sculptures which ornament the windows are such as this age could not make; they still actually exist." These 'palaces of the king' are mentioned by Diodôros in his epitome of Megasthenês, as will be seen by a reference to p. 39. It was in the interval which separates the journey of Fa-Hian from that of his compatriot Hiwen Thsâng—that is, between the year 400 and the year 632 after Christ—that the fall of Pâṭaliputra was accomplished, for where the splendid metropolis had once stood Hiwen Thsâng found nothing but ruins, and a village containing about two or three hundred houses. The cause of its downfall and decay is unknown. The ruins seen by the Chinese traveller are no longer visible, but lie buried deep below the foundations of modern Pâṭnâ. An excavation quite recently made in that city for the construction of a public tank placed this fact beyond question; for, when the workmen had dug down to a depth of 12 or 15 feet below the surface of the ground, some remains were discovered of what must have been the wooden wall spoken of by Megasthenês. I have received from a friend who inspected the excavation the following particulars of this interesting and remarkable discovery :—"During the cold season 1876, whilst digging a tank in Sheikh Mithia Ghari, a part of Pâṭnâ almost equally distant from the *chauk* (market-place) and the railway station, the excavators, at a depth of some 12 or 15 feet below the swampy surface, discovered the remains of a long brick wall running from N.W. to S.E. How far this wall extended beyond the limits of the excavation—probably more than a hundred yards—it is impossible to say. Not far from the wall, and almost parallel to it, was found a line of palisades; the strong timber of which it was composed inclined slightly towards the wall. In one place there appeared to have been some sort of outlet, for two wooden pillars rising to a height of some 8 or 9 feet above what had evidently been the ancient level of the place, and between which no trace of palisades could be discovered, had all the appearance of door or gate posts. A number of wells and sinks were also found, their mouths being in each case indicated by heaps of fragments of broken mud vessels. From the best-preserved specimens of these, it

the Helots as slaves, and these Helots do servile labour; but the Indians do not even use aliens as slaves, and much less a countryman of their own.

XI. But further: in India the whole people

---

appeared that their shape must have differed from that of those now in use. One of the wells having been cleared out, it was found to yield capital drinking water, and among the rubbish taken out of it were discovered several iron spear-heads, a fragment of a large vessel, &c." The fact thus established—that old Palibothra, and its wall with it, are deep underground—takes away all probability from the supposition of Ravenshaw that the large mounds near Pâṭnâ (called Panch-Pahâri, or 'five hills'), consisting of *débris* and bricks, may be the remains of towers or bastions of the ancient city. The identity of Pâṭaliputra with Pâṭnâ was a question not settled without much previous controversy. D'Anville, as has been already stated, misled by the assertion of Pliny that the Jomanes (Jamnâ) flows through the Palibothri into the Ganges, referred its site to the position of Allahâbâd, where these two rivers unite. Rennel, again, thought it might be identical with Kanauj, though he afterwards abandoned this opinion; while Wilford placed it on the left bank of the Ganges at some distance to the north of Râjmahâl, and Francklin at Bhâgalpûr. The main objection to the claims of Pâṭnâ—its not being situated at the confluence of any river with the Ganges—was satisfactorily disposed of when in the course of research it was brought to light that the Sôn was not only identical with the Erranoboas, but that up to the year 1379, when it formed a new channel for itself, it had joined the Ganges in the neighbourhood of Pâṭnâ. I may conclude this notice by quoting from Strabo a description of a procession such as Megasthenês (from whose work Strabo very probably drew his information) must have seen parading the streets of Palibothra:—"In processions at their festivals many elephants are in the train, adorned with gold and silver, numerous carriages drawn by four horses and by several pairs of oxen; then follows a body of attendants in full dress, (bearing) vessels of gold, large basins and goblets an *orguia* in breadth, tables, chairs of state, drinking-cups, and lavers of Indian copper, most of which were set with precious stones, as emeralds, beryls, and Indian carbuncles; garments embroidered and interwoven with gold; wild beasts, as buffaloes, panthers, tame lions; and a multitude of birds of variegated plumage and of fine song."—Bohn's Transl. of Strabo, III. p. 117.

are divided into about seven castes. Among these are the Sophists, who are not so numerous as the others, but hold the supreme place of dignity and honour,—for they are under no necessity of doing any bodily labour at all, or of contributing from the produce of their labour anything to the common stock, nor indeed is any duty absolutely binding on them except to perform the sacrifices offered to the gods on behalf of the state. If any one, again, has a private sacrifice to offer, one of these sophists shows him the proper mode, as if he could not otherwise make an acceptable offering to the gods. To this class the knowledge of divination among the Indians is exclusively restricted, and none but a sophist is allowed to practise that art. They predict about such matters as the seasons of the year, and any calamity which may befall the state; but the private fortunes of individuals they do not care to predict,—either because divination does not concern itself with trifling matters, or because to take any trouble about such is deemed unbecoming. But if any one fails thrice to predict truly, he incurs, it is said, no further penalty than being obliged to be silent for the future, and there is no power on earth able to compel that man to speak who has once been condemned to silence. These sages go naked, living during winter in the open air to enjoy the sunshine, and during summer, when the heat is too powerful, in meadows and low grounds under large trees, the shadow whereof Nearchos says extends to five plethra in circuit, adding that even ten thousand men* could be covered by the shadow of a single tree. They live upon the fruits which each season produces, and on the bark of trees,—the bark being no less sweet and nutritious than the fruit of the date-palm.

After these, the second caste consists of the tillers of the soil, who form the most numerous class of the population. They are neither furnished with arms, nor have any military duties to perform, but they cultivate the soil and pay tribute to the kings and the independent cities. In times of civil war the soldiers are not allowed to molest the husbandmen or ravage their lands: hence, while the former are fighting and killing each other as they can, the latter may be seen close at hand tranquilly pursuing their work,—perhaps ploughing, or gathering in their crops, pruning the trees, or reaping the harvest.

The third caste among the Indians consists of the herdsmen, both shepherds and neat-herds; and these neither live in cities nor in

---

* Cf. the description of the same tree quoted from Onesikritos, Strabo XV. i. 21. Cf. also Milton's description of it in *Paradise Lost*, bk. ix., ll. 1100 *et seqq.*:—

"There soon they chose
The fig-tree, not that kind for fruit renowned,
But such as at this day to Indians known
In Malabar or Deccan spreads her arms
Branching so broad and long that in the ground
The bended twigs take root, and daughters grow
About the mother tree, a pillared shade
High overarched, and echoing walks between."

villages, but they are nomadic and live on the hills. They too are subject to tribute, and this they pay in cattle. They scour the country in pursuit of fowl and wild beasts.

XII. The fourth caste consists of handicraftmen and retail-dealers. They have to perform gratuitously certain public services, and to pay tribute from the products of their labour. An exception, however, is made in favour of those who fabricate the weapons of war,—and not only so, but they even draw pay from the state. In this class are included shipbuilders, and the sailors employed in the navigation of the rivers.

The fifth caste among the Indians consists of the warriors, who are second in point of numbers to the husbandmen, but lead a life of supreme freedom and enjoyment. They have only military duties to perform. Others make their arms, and others supply them with horses, and they have others to attend on them in the camp, who take care of their horses, clean their arms, drive their elephants, prepare their chariots, and act as their charioteers. As long as they are required to fight they fight, and when peace returns they abandon themselves to enjoyment,—the pay which they receive from the state being so liberal that they can with ease maintain themselves and others besides.

The sixth class consists of those called superintendents. They spy out what goes on in country and town, and report everything to the king where the people have a king, and to the magistrates where the people are self-governed,† and it is against use and wont for these to give in a false report;—but indeed no Indian is accused of lying.

The seventh caste consists of the councillors of state, who advise the king, or the magistrates of self-governed cities, in the management of public affairs. In point of numbers this is a small class, but it is distinguished by superior wisdom and justice, and hence enjoys the prerogative of choosing governors, chiefs of provinces, deputy-governors, superintendents of the treasury, generals of the army, admirals of the navy, controllers, and commissioners who superintend agriculture.

The custom of the country prohibits intermarriage between the castes:—for instance, the husbandman cannot take a wife from the artizan caste, nor the artizan a wife from the husbandman caste. Custom also prohibits any one from exercising two trades, or from changing from one caste to another. One cannot, for instance, become a husbandman if he is a herdsman, or

---

† "There have always been extensive tracts without any common head, some under petty chiefs, and some formed of independent villages: in troubled times, also towns have often for a long period carried on their own government. All these would be called republics by the Greeks, who would naturally fancy their constitutions similar to what they had seen at home."—Elphinstone's *History of India*, p. 240.

become a herdsman if he is an artizan. It is permitted that the sophist only be from any caste: for the life of the sophist is not an easy one, but the hardest of all.

XIII. The Indians hunt all wild animals in the same way as the Greeks, except the elephant, which is hunted in a mode altogether peculiar, since these animals are not like any others. The mode may be thus described:—The hunters having selected a level tract of arid ground dig a trench all round it, enclosing as much space as would suffice to encamp a large army. They make the trench with a breadth of five fathoms and a depth of four. But the earth which they throw out in the process of digging they heap up in mounds on both edges of the trench, and use it as a wall. Then they make huts for themselves by excavating the wall on the outer edge of the trench, and in these they leave loopholes, both to admit light, and to enable them to see when their prey approaches and enters the enclosure. They next station some three or four of their best-trained she-elephants within the trap, to which they leave only a single passage by means of a bridge thrown across the trench, the framework of which they cover over with earth and a great quantity of straw, to conceal the bridge as much as possible from the wild animals, which might else suspect treachery. The hunters then go out of the way, retiring to the cells which they had made in the earthen wall. Now the wild elephants do not go near inhabited places in the day-time, but during the night-time they wander about everywhere, and feed in herds, following as leader the one who is biggest and boldest, just as cows follow bulls. As soon, then, as they approach the enclosure, and hear the cry and catch scent of the females, they rush at full speed in the direction of the fenced ground, and being arrested by the trench move round its edge until they fall in with the bridge, along which they force their way into the enclosure. The hunters meanwhile, perceiving the entrance of the wild elephants, hasten, some of them, to take away the bridge, while others, running off to the nearest villages, announce that the elephants are within the trap. The villagers, on hearing the news, mount their most spirited and best-trained, elephants, and as soon as mounted ride off to the trap; but, though they ride up to it, they do not immediately engage in a conflict with the wild elephants, but wait till these are sorely pinched by hunger and tamed by thirst; when they think their strength has been enough weakened, they set up the bridge anew and ride into the enclosure, when a fierce assault is made by the tame elephants upon those that have been entrapped, and then, as might be expected, the wild elephants, through loss of spirit and faintness from hunger, are overpowered. On this the hunters, dismounting from their elephants, bind with fetters the feet of the wild ones, now by this time quite exhausted. Then they instigate the tame ones to beat them with repeated blows, until their sufferings wear them out and they fall to the ground. The hunters meanwhile, standing near them, slip nooses over their necks and mount them while yet lying on the ground; and, to prevent them shaking off their riders, or doing mischief otherwise, make with a sharp knife an incision all round their neck, and fasten the noose round in the incision. By means of the wound thus made they keep their head and neck quite steady: for if they become restive and turn round, the wound is galled by the action of the rope. They shun, therefore, violent movements, and, knowing that they have been vanquished, suffer themselves to be led in fetters by the tame ones.

XIV. But such as are too young, or through the weakness of their constitution not worth keeping, their captors allow to escape to their old haunts; while those which are retained they lead to the villages, where at first they give them green stalks of corn and grass to eat. The creatures, however, having lost all spirit, have no wish to eat; but the Indians, standing round them in a circle, soothe and cheer them by chanting songs to the accompaniment of the music of drums and cymbals, for the elephant is of all brutes the most intelligent. Some of them, for instance, have taken up their riders when slain in battle and carried them away for burial; others have covered them, when lying on the ground, with a shield; and others have borne the brunt of battle in their defence when fallen. There was one even that died of remorse and despair because it had killed its rider in a fit of rage. I have myself actually seen an elephant playing on cymbals, while other elephants were dancing to his strains: a cymbal had been attached to each foreleg of the performer, and a third to what is called his trunk, and while he beat in turn the cymbal on his trunk he beat in proper time those on his two legs. The dancing elephants all the while kept dancing in a circle, and as they raised and curved their forelegs in turn they too moved in proper time, following as the musician led.

The elephant, like the bull and the horse, engenders in spring, when the females emit breath through the spiracles beside their temples, which open at that season. The period of gestation is at shortest sixteen months, and never exceeds eighteen. The birth is single, as in the case of the mare, and is suckled till it reaches its eighth year. The elephants that live longest attain an age of two hundred years, but many of them die prematurely of disease. If they die of sheer old age, however, the term of life is what has been stated. Diseases of their eyes are cured by pouring cows' milk into them, and other distempers by administering draughts of black wine; while their wounds are cured by the application of roasted pork. Such are the remedies used by the Indians.

XV. But the tiger the Indians regard as a much more powerful animal than the elephant. Nearchos tells us that he had seen the skin of a tiger, though the tiger itself he had not seen. The Indians, however, informed him that the tiger equals in size the largest horse, but that for swiftness and strength no other animal can be compared with it: for that the tiger, when it encounters the elephant, leaps up upon the head of the elephant and strangles it with ease; but that those animals which we ourselves see and call tigers are but jackals with spotted skins and larger than other jackals.‡ In the same way with regard to ants also, Nearchos says that he had not himself seen a specimen of the sort which other writers declared to exist in India, though he had seen many skins of them which had been brought into the Makedonian camp. But Megasthenês avers that the tradition about the ants is strictly true,—that they are gold-diggers, not for the sake of the gold itself, but because by instinct they burrow holes in the earth to lie in, just as the tiny ants of our own country dig little holes for themselves, only those in India being larger than foxes make their burrows proportionately larger. But the ground is impregnated with gold, and the Indians thence obtain their gold. Now Megasthenês writes what he had heard from hearsay, and as I have no ex-

‡ Leopards are meant.

acter information to give I willingly dismiss the subject of the ant.§ But about parrots N e a r c h o s writes as if they were a new curiosity, and tells us that they are indigenous to India, and what-like they are, and that they speak with a human voice; but since I have myself seen many parrots, and know others who are acquainted with the bird, I will say nothing about it as if it were still unfamiliar.|| Nor will I say aught of the apes, either touching their size, or the beauty which distinguishes them in India, or the mode in which they are hunted, for I should only be stating what is well known, except perhaps the fact that they are beautiful. Regarding snakes, too, N e a r c h o s tells us that they are caught in the country, being spotted, and nimble in their movements, and that one which P e i t h o the son of Antigenês caught measured about sixteen cubits, though the Indians allege that the largest snakes are much larger. But no cure of the bite of the Indian snake has been found out by any of the Greek physicians, though the Indians, it is certain, can cure those who have been bitten.¶ And Nearchos adds this, that A l e x a n d e r had all the most skilful of the Indians in the healing art collected around him, and had caused proclamation to be made throughout the camp that if

---

§ See notes to pp. 94 and 96.

|| Quis expedivit *psittaco* suum XAIRE.—Persius, Prol. to Sat. l. 8.

¶ This is, unfortunately, one of the lost arts.

any one were bitten he should repair to the royal tent; but these very same men were able to cure other diseases and pains also. With many bodily pains, however, the Indians are not afflicted, because in their country the seasons are genial. In the case of an attack of severe pain they consult the sophists, and these seemed to cure whatever diseases could be cured not without divine help.*

XVI. The dress worn by the Indians is made of cotton, as Nearchos tells us,—cotton produced from those trees of which mention has already been made.† But this cotton is either of a brighter white colour than any cotton found elsewhere, or the darkness of the Indian complexion makes their apparel look so much the whiter. They wear an under-garment of cotton which reaches below the knee halfway down to the ankles, and also an upper garment which they throw partly over their shoulders, and partly twist in folds round their head.‡ The Indians wear

* That is, by the use of charms: see Strabo XV. i. 45.

† A slip on the part of Arrian, as no previous mention has been made of the cotton-tree.

‡ "The valuable properties of the cotton-wool produced from the cotton-shrub (*Gossypium herbaceum*) were early discovered. And we read in Rig-veda hymns of 'Day and Night' like 'two famous female weavers' intertwining the extended thread......Cotton in its manufactured state was new to the Greeks who accompanied Alexander the Great to India. They describe Hindus as clothed in garments made from wool which grows on trees. One cloth, they say, reaches to the middle of the leg, whilst another is folded round the shoulders. Hindus still dress in the fashion thus described, which is also alluded to in old Sanskrit literature. In the frescoes on the caves of Ajanta this costume is carefully represented . . . . The cloth which Nearchus speaks of as reaching to the middle of the

also earrings of ivory, but only such of them do this as are very wealthy, for all Indians do not wear them. Their beards, Nearchos tells us, they dye of one hue and another, according to taste. Some dye their white beards to make them look as white as possible, but others dye them blue; while some again prefer a red tint, some a purple, and others a rank green.§ Such Indians, he also says, as are thought anything of, use parasols as a screen from the heat. They wear shoes made of white leather, and these are elaborately trimmed, while the soles are variegated, and made of great thickness, to make the wearer seem so much the taller.

I proceed now to describe the mode in which the Indians equip themselves for war, premising that it is not to be regarded as the only one in vogue. The foot-soldiers carry a bow made of equal length with the man who bears it. This they rest upon the ground, and pressing against it with their left foot thus discharge the arrow, having drawn the string far backwards: for the shaft they use is little short of being three

---

leg is the Dhotî. It is from 2½ to 3½ yards long by 2 to 3 feet broad......It is a costume much resembling that of a Greek statue, and the only change observable within 3,000 years is, that the Dhotî may now be somewhat broader and longer."—Mrs. Manning's *Ancient and Mediæval India*, vol. II. pp. 356-8.

§ Perhaps some of these colours were but transition shades assumed by the dye before settling to its final hue. The readers of Warren's *Ten Thousand a Year* will remember the plight of the hero of the tale when having dyed his hair he found it, chameleon-like, changing from hue to hue. This custom is mentioned also by Strabo.

yards long, and there is nothing which can resist an Indian archer's shot, — neither shield nor breastplate, nor any stronger defence if such there be. In their left hand they carry bucklers made of undressed ox-hide, which are not so broad as those who carry them, but are about as long. Some are equipped with javelins instead of bows, but all wear a sword, which is broad in the blade, but not longer than three cubits; and this, when they engage in close fight (which they do with reluctance), they wield with both hands, to fetch down a lustier blow. The horsemen are equipped with two lances like the lances called *saunia*, and with a shorter buckler than that carried by the foot-soldiers. But they do not put saddles on their horses, nor do they curb them with bits like the bits in use among the Greeks or the Kelts, but they fit on round the extremity of the horse's mouth a circular piece of stitched raw ox-hide studded with pricks of iron or brass pointing inwards, but not very sharp: if a man is rich he uses pricks made of ivory. Within the horse's mouth is put an iron prong like a skewer, to which the reins are attached. When the rider, then, pulls the reins, the prong controls the horse, and the pricks which are attached to this prong goad the mouth, so that it cannot but obey the reins.

XVII. The Indians are in person slender and tall, and of much lighter weight than other men.

The animals used by the common sort for riding on are camels and horses and asses, while the wealthy use elephants,—for it is the elephant which in India carries royalty.|| The conveyance which ranks next in honour is the chariot and four; the camel ranks third; while to be drawn by a single horse is considered no distinction at all.¶ But Indian women, if possessed of uncommon discretion, would not stray from virtue for any reward short of an elephant, but on receiving this a lady lets the giver enjoy her person. Nor do the Indians consider it any disgrace to a woman to grant her favours for an elephant, but it is rather regarded as a high compliment to the sex that their charms should be deemed worth an elephant. They marry without either giving or taking dowries, but the women, as soon as they are marriageable, are brought forward by their fathers and exposed in public, to be selected by the victor in wrestling or boxing or running, or by some one who excels in any other manly exercise.* The people of India live upon grain, and are tillers of the soil; but we must except the hillmen, who eat the flesh of beasts of chase.

|| Hence one of his names is Vârana, implying that he not only carries but protects his royal rider.

¶ The *ekka*, so common in the north-west of India, is no doubt here indicated.

* Marriage customs appear to have varied, as a reference to the extract from Strabo pp. 70-71 will show. See Wheeler's *History of India*, pp. 167-8.

It is sufficient for me to have set forth these facts regarding the Indians, which, as the best known, both Nearchos and Megasthenês, two men of approved character, have recorded. And since my design in drawing up the present narrative was not to describe the manners and customs of the Indians, but to relate how Alexander conveyed his army from India to Persia, let this be taken as a mere episode.